THE HOME FRONT
POCKET MANUAL 1939–1945

Edited by Lucinda Gosling

CASEMATE

Oxford & Philadelphia

Published in Great Britain and
the United States of America in 2020 by
CASEMATE PUBLISHERS
The Old Music Hall, 106–108 Cowley Road, Oxford OX4 1JE, UK
1950 Lawrence Road, Havertown, PA 19083, USA

Introduction and chapter introductory texts by Lucinda Gosling
© Casemate Publishers 2020

Hardback Edition: ISBN 978-1-61200-867-7
Digital Edition: ISBN 978-1-61200-868-4

A CIP record for this book is available from the British Library

Printed and bound in India by Replika Press Pvt. Ltd.

Typeset by Versatile PreMedia Services (P) Ltd

The information contained in the documents in this book is solely for historical interest
and does not constitute advice. The publisher accepts no liability for the consequences of
following any of the details in this book.

For a complete list of Casemate titles, please contact:

CASEMATE PUBLISHERS (UK)
Telephone (01865) 241249
Fax (01865) 794449
Email: casemate-uk@casematepublishers.co.uk
www.casematepublishers.co.uk

CASEMATE PUBLISHERS (US)
Telephone (610) 853-9131
Fax (610) 853-9146
Email: casemate@casematepublishers.com
www.casematepublishers.com

CONTENTS

INTRODUCTION

The outbreak of war between Britain and Germany, when it was announced at 11:15am on 3 September 1939, was greeted by the British people with a mix of emotions, but with very little surprise. Unlike the Great War twenty years earlier which had crept up on the unsuspecting population, the inevitability of this conflict meant Neville Chamberlain's speech concluding with the words, 'this country is at war with Germany', broadcast into thousands of homes around the country, was largely met with grim acceptance.

In 1933, Adolf Hitler had become Chancellor of Germany, establishing a one-party state under the Nazis and exploiting a nationalist desire to reverse the humiliating penalties imposed on Germany following the end of the First World War. Hitler's policy was marked by aggressive territorial expansion, first the reoccupation of the Rhineland, followed two years later by Austria and then demands that the Sudetenland area of Czechoslovakia, populated by a German-speaking population, become a part of Germany. The British did not want war, and nor did their Prime Minister, Neville Chamberlain. He had done as much as he could to avoid it, travelling to Germany at the end of September 1938 and returning having been a signatory to the Munich Agreement, which, by allowing Hitler to annexe Czech territories, alleviated the immediate threat of war and gave Britain, and her ally France, breathing space to rearm and plan for a conflict that was still a distinct possibility. Although Chamberlain's policy of appeasement, and his famous proclamation of 'peace in our time' offered a glimmer of hope amid the gathering clouds, less than a year later, on 1 September 1939, Hitler invaded Poland. Bound by a guarantee made in March to defend Polish independence, Britain and France declared war on Germany two days later.

Even before the official announcement of war, a blackout order had been implemented, plunging most British citizens into darkness for the first time, though there had already been a trial blackout in London on 9 August. In parks, the trenches that had been dug the previous year were beginning to look as if they might be needed as protection from the bombs that were expected to rain from the sky imminently. And just minutes after the radio broadcast, the eerie wail of the siren started up, a sound that would soon become all-too familiar to millions. There was no doubt that this would be a war that would affect all of society. This would be a people's war.

For the next six years of war, the population would fight not only on land, air and sea around the globe, but at home too, as the country shared in the sacrifices and privations impacting nearly every aspect of daily life. The defendants of this domestic battlefront were largely women, a fact fully recognised by the government. As one Ministry of Information leaflet summarised:

Many vital decisions for the home front have been taken by the Ministers of the Crown for the whole nation; but the housewives have had the task of translating national economy into domestic practice.

The country's ceaseless drive to exercise economy, to scrimp, save, reuse, repurpose and generally make do and mend, would dominate many women's lives on the home front. There were myriad responsibilities all focused on the war effort; the public were continually reminded that however small the action, the collective effect would be a crucial contribution towards eventual victory.

The initial priority in the first weeks of war was preservation of life. Citizens were quickly made aware of their key responsibilities – strict observance of the blackout rules; the carrying of gas masks at all times, and the understanding that they must seek shelter on hearing the air raid siren. Public information leaflets were distributed periodically with clear instructions for the population, who were also advised to listen to the BBC broadcasts for further information. Places where large numbers of people could congregate, such as theatres and cinemas, were closed with immediate effect to minimise the possibility of mass casualties in the event of a direct hit (they would later re-open) and, most sobering, families were instructed to ensure each member was labelled with their name and address for identification purposes. It is notable that in preparation for expected casualties, the government had stockpiled coffins but, while the numbers of civilians killed in air raids was devastating, it did not reach anticipated levels and during the Blitz it was the huge numbers of people made homeless by the raids that provided the government with the biggest challenge.

On 1 September, at the same time the blackout was first implemented, a leaflet entitled, *What to Do in an Air Raid* was delivered to British homes, advising people to seek protection in public shelters (which could be any hastily adapted building from town halls to railway stations), and to give instructions on how to find protection in the home. The first major disruption of the war was not only logistical, but also highly emotive, as the decision was taken to evacuate city-dwelling children to places of safety in the country, a plan that had been mooted throughout the decade, but was finally crystallised in form when a Committee of Evacuation was set up in May 1938. The scheme was outlined in the third public information leaflet to be distributed and promised parents that householders in the countryside were willing and able to provide homes for children from urban areas. This logistically ambitious scheme transported 1.5 million children (against a planned 3.5 million), as well as mothers with infants or toddlers, disabled people, teachers and helpers. When the expected air raids did not materialise during what became known as the 'phoney war', most evacuees returned to their homes, although there would be another exodus when the Luftwaffe began their bombing campaign from

September 1940. Air raids meant for many the misery of nights spent in either public shelters, damp Anderson shelters or in a basement, most of which were uncomfortable and inconvenient. Many people, unable to tolerate one more night of discomfort, chose to remain in their beds, or at least downstairs in their homes, considering a good night's sleep worth the risk.

Another stricture communicated early in the war was to strongly advise against stockpiling food before a fair scheme to ensure equal distribution could be implemented. Rationing was introduced in January 1940 with butter, bacon and sugar the first foods to be limited. Meat and preserves were rationed soon afterwards, in March, followed by tea, margarine and cooking fats in July. Other foodstuffs would be rationed over time; cereal, biscuits, canned fruit, rice, chocolate and other sweets. Not all foods were rationed, but what was not was invariably in short supply and queuing soon became a feature of every shopping trip. Some non-perishable items were distributed via a points system, with each person allocated sixteen points every month. This continued scarcity of everyday foods would test the home cook's resourcefulness and ingenuity to its limits, but the Ministry of Food, headed by Lord Woolton, was there to support those who fed the nation with tips and ideas distributed via leaflets and advertisements. A series of 'Food Facts' advertisements, numbered from 1 to 24 appeared in newspapers and magazines, with advice that ranged from the generic ('Never eat more than enough') to what might be considered culinary eccentricity. The aim was to support housewives. Not only was it important to save food and avoid waste, but in the aftermath of the First World War, studies into the nation's nutrition had

MINISTRY OF FOOD

THE WEEK'S

FOOD

FACTS N° 3

Start now to collect these useful advertisements. Pin them up in your kitchen.

PLEASE make full use of the fruit and vegetables now so plentiful. It is important that we should eat home produce rather than food which has to come from overseas. *Never* waste anything, however small. *Never* eat more than enough. You'll be fitter, you'll save money, you'll make cargo space available for materials of war. *Every time you cook you can help or hinder Hitler!*

ON THE KITCHEN FRONT

HEALTH HINT. Among the protective foods, *salads* have a high place. Eat a salad every day while they are so plentiful.

BUTTER PAPER. Always scrape the paper in which butter or margarine has been wrapped. The papers themselves should be saved for greasing baking dishes or covering food while it is cooking in the oven.

REMEMBER that a plate of fresh home-grown fruit (plums for example) makes a refreshing dish. It will save fuel and will help to cut down the nation's consumption of imported food. *You can hear other useful time-and-fuel-saving hints on the wireless each morning at 8.15.*

RECIPE for Vegetable Hot-pot
Prepare and cut into convenient pieces ½ lb. potatoes, ¼ lb. carrots, ¼ lb. onions and ¼ lb. turnips. Put into a saucepan with a teacupful of hot water, put on the lid, bring to the boil and cook for 15 minutes. Then add a teacupful of shelled peas, ¼ lb. tomatoes and a few sprigs of mint, season with salt and pepper, put on the lid again and cook for 20 minutes more. Strain off the liquid which can be used in preparing a parsley sauce to serve with the vegetables.

Another way : If an ounce of dripping or margarine can be spared it should be melted in the saucepan and the vegetables tossed in it before the water is added to the pan. This much improves the flavour of the hot-pot.

Save food, spare cargo-space, save money !

THE MINISTRY OF FOOD, LONDON, S.W.1

7

laid the foundations of a state-sponsored campaign to improve Britain's health by a better, more varied diet. With good nutrition now directly linked to health and strength, ensuring a well-nourished nation on limited supplies was the primary aim of the Ministry of Food. Growing (or foraging) food was encouraged as a way to augment rationed meals with more plentiful, wholesome and vitamin-rich vegetables.

Food was not the only commodity limited to the British people. As the war continued, it seemed there were shortages of everything from petrol, furniture and kitchen utensils to textiles for new clothing. Clothes rationing came into effect on 1 June 1941 and allowed each adult 66 coupons a year, an allocation that had to be carefully managed, even more so when they were then reduced to 44 per person per year in 1943. Recognising that children tended to have growth spurts, they were given extra coupons and clothing exchanges, where outgrown clothes could be traded, became another essential service. The number of coupons available continued to fluctuate, with the lowest point between September 1945 and April 1946 when each person was allowed only 24 coupons. With a suit or outdoor coat taking up 18 coupons, and a wool dress 11, finding imaginative ways to stretch a clothing ration became just as essential as suggestions for making the most of rationed food. Advice on sewing, knitting, darning, mending, clothing upkeep and adapting old, worn-out clothes in order to magically transform them into new garments was liberally disseminated.

Clothes were still expensive; in fact, more expensive than before the war. A man's shirt was five points, whether it was from a village draper or Harrods, meaning that the more wealthy could afford to buy better quality, and longer-lasting clothes, this in addition to the store of well-made clothes they were already likely to be able to draw on. The introduction of the Utility range of clothing in 1942, with prototypes designed by members of the Incorporated Society of London Fashion Designers, among them Norman Hartnell and Victor Stiebel, ensured there was an adequate supply of quality clothes which were not only economical, but fashionable too. This egalitarian approach helped towards creating a fairer system, giving the less well-off a chance to buy something new and stylish at a reasonable cost. Rationing might be grumbled about but in general the public accepted that such measures were necessary; mass observation reports confirmed that 70% of the population approved of the rationing policy and believed that putting up with a lack of clothes, or smaller portions of food, was a necessary inconvenience, and all part of the war effort.

The Second World War was a conflict in which communication played an essential role in galvanising the home front into this effort, and it came in many forms – radio broadcasts, propaganda and public information posters, leaflets, booklets, demonstrations, newspaper articles, newsreels and magazines. Women's magazines in particular were a rich source of information and an effective conduit of government advice. In fact, they were considered so effective, several women's

8

magazines were recruited as a vehicle for home front propaganda with a committee established comprised of editors from leading publications. Information channelled through the pages of a favourite magazine, imparted with a sensitivity and knowledge of its readership, had a greater chance of engaging women than a standard leaflet intended for a more generic audience. The magazine format also allowed for finer detail and nuance, and with pages to fill, every conceivable aspect of wartime life was tackled by feature writers from feeding pets to rubbing raw potato on suits to counteract shine. At the same time, magazines could also choose to devote a proportion of column inches to articles that ignored the war completely. Romantic stories or thrillers, movie star news as well as the latest fashions, all allowed temporary escapism and respite from the hardships of wartime life.

Britannia & Eve magazine had launched on 1 May 1929, a merger of two separate titles. *Eve*, a high-quality women's magazine with the by-line 'The Lady's Pictorial', had been in publication since 1926, while *Britannia*, aimed at a more unisex audience, had been published throughout 1928. As part of a publishing group that also included *The Illustrated London News*, *The Sphere* and *The Sketch*, the monthly magazine, consisting of roughly 125 pages, attracted a roster of quality contributors, combining intelligent opinion pieces, general interest features, short stories by some of the leading writers of the day and articles on fashion, family, the home, health, beauty, but also motoring, careers and education. Its target market was aspirational middle-class and upper middle-class women, indicated not only by its cover price, which in 1939 was 1 shilling, but also references to an affluent pre-war existence in wartime articles; how to do without servants or a laundry service for instance. *Britannia & Eve*, with its varied subject matter and edifying articles positioned itself somewhere between high fashion magazines such as *Harper's Bazaar* or *Vogue* and the cheaper women's weekly magazines like *Woman* or *Woman's Own*.

Other magazines in the same stable as *Britannia & Eve* were also finding their usual editorial approach needed to bend to wartime conditions. *The Tatler*, the bible of high society had been in weekly publication since 1901 and mixed photographs and gossip about the upper classes with features on fashion, travel, theatre, entertainment and a rich seam of illustration. During the First World War it had optimistically spent the first few weeks of the conflict declaring itself a refuge from the unpleasantness of it all but eventually found its own role, offering cartoons to keep soldiers smiling together with news on what society types were doing towards the war effort. It followed a similar formula in 1939, absorbing another title, *The Bystander*, when paper shortages required its sacrifice. Alongside reports on stately homes requisitioned for war activities and pictures of lords, ladies and minor royals in uniform, there were also more practical articles. After all, even the wealthy, well-heeled *Tatler* reader needed some guidance in how to cope. *The Illustrated Sporting and Dramatic News*, first published in 1879, had a more unisex readership, and offered suggestions for correspondingly unisex problems such as safe wartime motoring, food for dogs or vegetable gardening.

As well as practical advice, there was a role for magazines to play when it came to keeping morale on an even keel. *Britannia & Eve* was no exception. It championed the housewife, or the woman who stayed at home, and emphasised the important role she could play in the war effort:

> We can't all be in the Services. We can't all make munitions or be Red Cross nurses. Plenty of us, for various reasons, cannot even leave the shelter of our own homes to do an outright job of work towards winning the war. But every woman in this country can go through the war with her head held high in the knowledge that, within her scope, she has given of her best, and that to the noble sacrifices which have been made, she can at least offer the tribute of a clear conscience. (June, 1942)

Such pep talks were a regular feature in the magazine, given as a mother, sister or friend might do, or perhaps, a kindly if opinionated headmistress. The magazine also knew where people's weak spots lay and often asked readers to examine their conscience when it came to personal sacrifices. 'Refuse that little bit of extra food sometimes offered on the quiet. Ask yourself – ask anybody: "Why should any one person have more than her neighbour?"' suggested one writer in September 1941, a point at which food rationing had really begun to bite. And for those who were feeling frustrated at the dearth of silk stockings, they were reminded that, 'Silk goes towards an airman's parachute', and, as for the lack of knicker elastic, '30lb of rubber saved goes to make an escape dinghy.' Magazines like *Britannia & Eve* shared in the trials and tribulations of a wartime existence, it sympathised, but at the same time briskly refused to indulge mopers and moaners. Readers, like the rest of the nation, were told to keep their chin up and carry on. Keeping up appearances was considered a patriotic duty ('I am just being defeatist if I turn myself into a drab dowd') and the magazine, to its credit, continued to put a positive spin on the shortages. Pared-down dress designs due to rationing were declared 'clean-cut elegance' and when rayon stockings were introduced as an alternative to silk, the magazine announced 'The British manufacturer would not let us down in the matter of stockings. Unlike the Nazi frau, the Englishwoman has a leg worth fighting for.' Dowdiness was to be avoided at all costs, and a practical solution could be found to almost every problem. It is notable that for the duration of the war, *Britannia & Eve* relocated its office, usually based in Inveresk House in Aldwych in the heart of London, to King's Langley in rural Hertfordshire. They were evacuees, like so many others.

As a monthly magazine, *Britannia & Eve* took some time to get out of the starting blocks in turning its attention to the war. There were only a couple of indications of the situation in the October issue, which most likely had much of its contents already planned out. An advertisement for Liberty's advised customers of changed opening hours, and Jean Burnup, the women's editor, explained that she had visited the Paris fashion shows just before war was declared. With a resigned air she wrote, 'Still having by us two of the pages that weren't scrapped while this issue of *Britannia & Eve* was being amended, we thought you might care to see some of the clothes that women might have been wearing if it hadn't happened.'

It was not until November that the magazine became more fully focused on the war. To Mary Young's regular column, 'Guide to a Pleasanter Life' was added the suffix, 'Even Now'; there was a spread on women volunteering with the W.V.S.; a cookery feature entitled, 'Making a Little Go a Long Way'; and another article that suggested some items to purchase in the face of wartime conditions – a large, comfortable fold-out lounge seat, suitable for shelters, 'for those lucky enough to have them,' and a three in one saucepan to save on gas. While advising thrift and economy, *Britannia & Eve* clung fiercely in the final months before rationing to the notion of living well when the opportunity presented itself. The December 1939 issue, featured recipes for a lavish Christmas dinner. The introductory text had a defiant tone: 'Come into the kitchen – and forget about the war. That's the Christmas spirit on the Home Front this year.'

In the same issue, Jean Burnup presented a fashion page hopefully announcing that after an initial scurry to stock up on, 'garments synonymous with warm usefulness and durability', the next phase of wartime fashions would be, 'gay, exciting and feminine'. There were still advertisements for Ballito silk stockings, but within a few months, they were replaced by those for uniforms for the women's services and Sanatogen or Ovaltine to help steady 'war nerves'.

Throughout the war years, the energy and vigour with which *Britannia & Eve* continued to dole out advice and ideas for its readers is impressive, though it is difficult to imagine anyone who followed its advice to the letter ever had time to sleep. Making do and mending was an intensively full-time job with a never-ending to-do list designed to extend the life of possessions and avoid any waste. There were features on repairing your fur coat, salvaging paper or scraps of fabric, keeping rabbits, regularly circulating bed sheets or carpets so they did not wear in the same place, wallpapering, repairing furniture, wartime car maintenance, how to cook with dried eggs, making slippers out of string or felt, cleaning the interior of your handbag all the while ensuring your nails were neat and polished, hair groomed, lipstick and powder present, and clothes brushed and pressed. It is exhausting just reading it.

It is also interesting, perplexing even from a 21st-century perspective, that the magazine rarely touches on the experiences of men who were serving in the armed forces. There were occasional articles on the current state of the war, and even on key military figures. But there was very little that touched on front-line action, or the ever-present possibility of widowhood. Women's magazines tended to steer clear of anything considered unpleasant, though this may have also been a conscious editorial decision, especially as *Britannia & Eve* was part of a publishing group in which two other magazines, *The Illustrated London News* and *The Sphere*, were focused almost entirely on the conflict itself. Fighting men are only mentioned in connection with returning home (when wives and sweethearts were told how to 'stay lovely for him'), in terms of relationship challenges or in advertisements for uniform, one of the few aspects in which a female partner might have had some influence. Equally, the magazine's occasional insistence on showing the 'latest fashions' when in reality, most of their readers would have no chance of ever procuring such sartorial delights, appears a conflicted approach, though these articles were usually counterbalanced by those that gave suggestions on how to save clothing coupons, or encouragement to try economical knitting patterns. It seems most likely that readers still enjoyed looking, even if owning the latest evening gown was just a fantasy. *Britannia & Eve* also tackled what we might consider thorny subjects; there are articles asking if this was the right time to have a baby, the complications that might arise from sharing a home with a friend, and many, such as, 'Aimlessness – Malady of the War,' confronting what were essentially mental health issues.

Despite advertisements that continued to explain about shortages, there was a tone of muted celebration to the first peacetime issues in the summer of 1945. In June's *Britannia & Eve*, Jane Gordon, in her regular On and Off-Duty column enthused about the imminent arrival of post-war nail varnishes from America by Cutex, which promised to be better and brighter than ever before. An illustration of a June bride graced the front cover and inside, Jean Burnup allowed herself the now unfamiliar thrill of suggesting designer frocks by Norman Hartnell, Rahvis, Worth and Jacqmar for brides, a stylish choice with longevity. There were also opinion pieces by C. Patrick Thompson. 'What Next in Britain' looked at the post-war political landscape and predicted the possible outcome of the next general election and in July, in an article on the concept of 'Pleasure' he ruminated on the changes war had brought about:

> World War II has blasted away a whole series of material and psychological barriers, expanded frontiers, lifted horizons and, incidentally, increased career and job possibilities.

Britannia & Eve magazine ran until 1957, long enough to see out the tail-end of rationing in Britain. It remains a richly fascinating resource for anyone interested in the home front experience during the Second World War, offering a feminine perspective which includes but also looks beyond purely domestic matters. In attitude it reflects the tenacity and stoicism of a society that endured sometimes unimaginable stresses and conditions, and alongside practical tips, there is an undercurrent of positive thinking as a way of winning over human weakness. Above all, magazines of this time tell us how, when tested, people can adapt and get by on very little; the habits of the home front are worth re-learning today as we face the global challenges resulting from what we have become – a throwaway society. The following excerpts, most taken from *Britannia & Eve* with others from *The Tatler, The Illustrated London News* and *The Illustrated Sporting & Dramatic News,* give an insight into those details of everyday life, of the challenges the nation faced and some of the solutions offered. They bring into sharp focus the extent to which every citizen contributed to the war effort, a fact summarised by the magazine in July 1943:

> It is her privilege – to be a woman at home in this war and by her perseverance and ingenuity in the daily routine of housekeeping, to make her quiet but vital contribution to victory.

CHAPTER I
HOME AND FAMILY

Disruption to home life was inevitable and unavoidable across almost every household in Britain due to war. In a broadcast by the Prime Minister in 1939, Chamberlain expressed empathy over this upheaval saying, 'I know well that in a greater or lesser degree the war has interrupted and affected your daily life… Most of these hardships and inconveniences have been brought about by the necessity of providing against attacks from the air.' Although the first months of the war would not bring the anticipated aerial attacks it was only a matter of time and at the war's end, over one million homes had been destroyed during air raids, with an unrecorded number suffering some level of damage. Protecting the home against German bombers was fundamental to war preparations and although the Anderson shelter, consisting of two corrugated sheets bolted together and sunk three feet into the earth, is synonymous with air raid protection on the domestic front, even during the height of the Blitz it was estimated that just over a quarter of home-owners were using them. Adapting a cellar, under stairs cupboard or downstairs room to offer both comfort and protection in the event of a blast became an alternative, though in truth no type of shelter could survive a direct hit. As early as July 1939, the first public information leaflet had been distributed to households, outlining what to do in the event of an air raid, detailing responsibilities such as fitting blackout curtains, cloths or shutters and ensuring buckets of water, earth and sand were always at hand in order to extinguish fire caused by incendiary bombs. Magazine advice went further, stressing details that would ameliorate the discomforts of raids, such as investing in a small electric stove to allow for simple meals and cups of tea during air raids.

Knowing your local ARP (Air Raid Precaution) warden was advisable, and each household was required to provide wardens with information on how many people occupied each home. An information card, stressing the key points to remember and with space to write who and where the nearest warden was, would ideally be hung up in a visible spot at home. Some people, especially those who lived in flats or did not have gardens, used public shelters, the conditions of which were variable but improved over time. Pets were not allowed in public shelters and it was advised that they be given a sedative during raids; aspirin was suggested, or advertisements for Bob Martin's Fit and Hysteria Powders were regularly placed in *Britannia & Eve* magazine.

Life below Stairs

Britannia & Eve (November 1940)

At this stage most of us have worked out a private security technique, something best suited to our own households and personal needs. Just the same, winter will bring the need for adaptations, so that our comfort and security in air raids may be brought into line with new conditions.

Moreover, it is essential to give a more permanent character to A.R.P. arrangements in the home. So far, many of us will have been content with improvised beds and other hastily concocted comforts, but cold winter nights demand something better, and it is wise to make plans for the whole winter.

Health, peace of mind, the vitality essential to stick it out depends on the manner in which we prepare ourselves for the coming winter's trials. It is safe to assume, even after the experiences of the past weeks, that we can and shall get accustomed to the strange conditions into which we are forced. Already people are finding it more and more possible to sleep under conditions that would formerly have seemed intolerable. Such is human adaptability, and we owe ourselves the benefit of all comfort that can be conceived in such difficult times.

To protect the occupants from falling plaster and shattered glass these shelters have been built on either side of the chimney breast. The sloping top is sandbagged and covered in with wood. A mattress and cushions are fitted on the floor of each.

Many who have used outdoor shelters during the finer weather will be forced by the winter into a compromise between shelter in the house and out of it. That is to say the strongest shelter will be reserved for use only in periods of imminent danger, while a protected room in the house will be used for the safer intervals so far as they can be judged.

To secure the maximum comfort and the minimum of dislocation to the home routine it is advisable for every home to adapt a downstairs room for shelter and sleeping purposes. If this is done with thoroughness, the room need not be divided from its original purpose.

In our illustration [page 16] we have pictured a sitting room as it was and again as it might be after adaptation. If structural reinforcement can be given to the room so much the better, but the sketch deals only with the comfort aspect.

An infallible blackout is the first need. Apart from regulations, it adds much to peace of mind if the windows can be screened quickly, easily and faultlessly.

Ventilation, too, must be considered. If the room is to be used indefinitely as a sleeping apartment, health demands fresh air. There are few better ways than the plywood shutter which fits the window frame giving a complete blackout and a slatted ventilator cut in the face of it to admit fresh air.

It may be necessary to remove incidental furniture from the room. Overcrowding must be avoided at all costs, but you will certainly need to introduce one or two new pieces, if comfort and convenience are to be served.

A wardrobe from upstairs will hold changes of clothing, warm coats and thick shoes in case of need. There should also be extra blankets and toilet necessities. Make your refuge room complete in its equipment so that you need leave it for no purpose whatsoever.

Sleeping accommodation must vary according to need and the shape and size of the room concerned, but if it is to keep its daytime character, a divan bed with a fitted day cover is the obvious choice.

If more than two people are to occupy the room—there may be children to consider—tiered bunks offer a good solution, without elaborate structural difficulty.

Overleaf is a corner of the adapted room showing the windows fitted with painted plywood shutters in which ventilator slats have been cut. The settee is replaced by a divan and screen, and here is a small cupboard with simple cooking necessities and a table lamp to replace overhead fixtures.

It is not a difficult matter to fit two bunks into a recess on an inside wall. Even the recess can be dispensed with. Curtains on swing rods are fitted to conceal the bunks during the day

Here is a sitting-room which is to be converted to the uses of an indoor shelter without too seriously disturbing its original function.

A recess on an inside wall is the best place to fit them, but if no recess is available, they can be built against any inside wall as shown in our sketch, where curtains on swing rods are suggested as a screen by day.

Overhead lighting fixtures should be removed, and, in fact, all inessential china and glass that could conceivably splinter or set up a nerve-racking giggle when the guns begin to bark.

An emergency light of some sort is a good thing to have by. Paraffin lamps are not advisable, but a small electric battery lamp such as is made for bedside use will do, and there are always candles.

A small cupboard with simple apparatus for heating water, milk and light food should not be omitted. A cup of tea and a snack will help to pass a long night, and if restoratives should happen to be needed, the same apparatus may prove invaluable. Keep a vessel of water always ready, and cover it to protect it from dust.

Official quarters inform us that the effects of blast are somewhat minimised by leaving doors and windows open. Open windows in winter are obviously impracticable, but the door of your shelter-room can be hung with a heavy curtain or a felt across the opening to defeat draught.

The sketch on the previous page shows a practical indoor shelter that can be erected without heavy cost or trouble, and does afford some further security inside the house without being too unsightly.

In each recess on either side of the chimney-breast a wooden structure with strong supporting sides and a forward sloping roof is fixed. Thick wood is used, and the "roof" is sandbagged and covered in with painted matchwood.

Inside each shelter a mattress and cushions are laid upon the floor, with warm rugs for covering. Two people can rest comfortably in each shelter with a reassuring measure of safety from splintered glass and the less serious forms of flying debris.

Unless your outdoor shelter is of a substantial kind, some indoor refuge of this kind will prove to be invaluable during the winter ahead. Some disorganisation of your household must result from the change, but not even the most house-proud have time for squeamishness on this score now.

With coal in short supply as early as November 1939, the householder's responsibility to exercise economy and limit the consumption of fuel was imperative to the war effort. Whereas coal could be rationed, managing the public use of gas and electricity was more difficult so a campaign to encourage fuel frugality was implemented. Country dwellers were urged to collect sticks and logs for fuel, and those with open fires were advised to use them not only to keep warm but for cooking; nestling casseroles or a kettle on a trivet close to the flames. Cooks were told to prepare and cook meals in bulk, filling the oven rather than wasting fuel on just one pot. The same principle applied to other household tasks such as ironing or washing up. In 1942, the government implemented another fuel-saving scheme introducing the 'five inches of water' rule for anyone taking a bath.

Fuel Facts

Britannia & Eve (February 1942)

Every woman can do a practical, vital job of work for the war effort by saving fuel this winter. There are direct and indirect ways of doing it and here are some of them.

Take the more obvious measures first:

If you live in the country collect wood and logs. At this time of the year there is plenty of it laying around. It is slightly damp, but not much the worst for that because it burns slowly. Use it in conjunction with coal. Use up every scrap of coal dust in the cellar. Damp it down a little and feed the fire with it along with lumps of coal. When you are going out, make the fire up with dust and well-sifted cinders.

A gas poker affords a quick and economical way of kindling fires. It does away with the need for wood and paper and consumes only a small quantity of gas.

Be economical with hot water in your home. This may not seem to have much connection with the fuel situation, but it has. If you keep a domestic boiler going two hours longer in order to provide more hot water for household purposes you use more fuel to do it.

Don't run the hot-water tap too freely. Make the best use of every drop. Save the washing up so it can be done in one swoop and with one measure of hot water. Use a little less water in your bath. If everyone in the household does this it may mean many gallons of hot water per day saved, with the commensurate amount of fuel.

To save gas and electric current make more general use of open fires for cooking. When you are alone in the house keep a large kettle of water on a trivet by the fire. Take water from this when you want it. As it is already half way to boiling you save quite an appreciable amount of gas in heating it up on the cooker. When making a stew bring the saucepan to the boil, then keep it simmering for the rest of the time on the trivet before the fire. This is more than economy of fuel, it is also good cooking.

Electric current can be saved in different small ways without notable inconvenience.

In the lavatory and bathroom, in the hall and passages, exchange hundred-watt bulbs for sixties or even forties. Except for close work or in sitting-rooms and bedrooms these should be sufficient.

Replace light bulbs in use with new ones if they have been in service for a long time. This pays. The older the bulb is the more current it uses.

Make use of all household electrical appliances carefully. For instance, don't heat up the electric iron to press one collar if you can possibly avoid it. Save up bits of ironing and make one lot of current do for several things.

Never boil more water in the electric kettle than you really need. A large kettle of water for one cup of tea is just waste. If you use a gas cooker don't turn up the flame so that it flares around the sides of the kettle. You don't get more heat this way but you use more gas.

Once a kettle or saucepan has reached the boil turn down the gas. The contents of the pot can be kept at boiling on a very low jet.

Before 1914, an estimated 12% of the female population was employed in domestic service. The First World War was significant in being the catalyst for a mass exodus of servants leaving their employers for jobs in war-related industries. Many of them never returned. Between the wars, most upper-class families had continued to employ some form of home help depending on their own circumstances, and even comfortable middle-class families might have a cook, a nanny, or at least a char-lady. In addition to this, external services such as laundries, and a boom in labour-saving household appliances, took away some of the most onerous of household tasks and had effectively replaced the post-war shortfall in available servants.

For the more affluent readers of *Britannia & Eve* magazine, the loss of home helps, whatever form they had taken, left them in a position where they were required to manage all domestic arrangements alone during wartime. Even in homes that had never known the luxury of servants, the absence of fathers, brothers and husbands, who would have carried out the traditionally masculine tasks of decorating, building, mending and car upkeep was felt keenly. *Britannia & Eve* magazine understood these predicaments and offered all kinds of practical advice from how to mend a fuse or a mangle, to decorating a room or mending a broken chair leg.

The perceived importance of 'keeping up appearances' at home saw a raft of articles on how to ensure everything was spick and span, with an emphasis on prolonging the life of household items. After all, it was highly unlikely worn-out linens, furniture or carpets could be replaced. For women who felt overwhelmed by this mountain of relentless tasks expected of them, *Britannia & Eve* helpfully published to-do lists and weekly schedules to help women navigate the labyrinth of domestic demands.

No Maid? No Matter!

Britannia & Eve (August 1943)

Starts at the beginning of the week with a meal list and a schedule of Week's Special Tasks and How To Fit Them In. This keeps everything orderly and sets the time-table working for the week.

Washes silver and glass that hasn't been stored away, in hot soapy water and ammonia to save polishing. Has varnished floor-surrounds long since and now only has to mop.

Shops before ten-thirty and on wash-day puts the clothes in water to soak before going out. This loosens the dirt and makes the final washing much easier. Irons, if possible, on the same day.

Reserves Friday afternoon for cooking as much food as possible for the week-end. Pastry, pudding and cakes can be completely cooked ; stews or meat pies and vegetables prepared for the oven.

Has cut out arduous furniture polishing and merely goes over polished surfaces at regular intervals with a chamois leather wrung out in tepid water mixed with a strong dash of vinegar.

Still entertains as far as the food situation will allow, but when more than two are invited always provides a buffet meal. This way food is prepared in advance and guests serve themselves.

Organises the family to help in lightening work by making their own beds, cleaning the bath and tidying bathroom litter after every use ; washing their own used china and cutlery after meals.

Scrubs kitchen table-top and other white-wood surfaces with salt and water, or with Parazone, a liquid bleaching agent obtainable at most stores, which keeps them white with little labour.

Polishes windows inside and out with Sposs, which is simply applied to windows and mirror surfaces on a soft cloth and leaves a clean and lustrous surface in a few seconds. Most stores have it.

Serious strip showing some of the current labour-saving of a housewife who does all her own work.

22

Home Savers

By Winifred Lewis

Britannia & Eve (February 1942)

Any woman can keep a beautiful home when she can go out and buy new things to replace shabby ones. The war has put an end to all that and it takes considerable thought and care to keep up a high standard in the home without replacements.

We don't pretend to deal in magic or promise to tell you how to give perpetual life to furnishings, but the several practical suggestions discussed below may help you to fend off the growing shabbiness of household things, and to keep them looking youthful into their middle age.

Carpets and Rugs

Shabby carpets make shabby rooms. Carpets are expensive things, anyway, even if you could get new ones; but daily care will help to keep the ones you've got in a good-looking mood.

All-over patterns are easiest to handle, because they show defects less readily, but don't give up hope, even if you have got those plain carpets which seemed so good when they were new.

Make a point of turning carpets around every few months if possible. This way, the wear is more evenly distributed, and it is much longer before you get those bare patches between the door and the fireplace, and at other points where the wear is hardest.

In a dining-room, or in any sitting-room where food is habitually served, watch that path between the doorway and the table. This is where food is often slopped on to the carpet, making a dirty track. Never bring food into the room, or take it out, without using a tray. It is a small matter, but it saves carpets.

Spread newspaper, or an old dust-sheet, over the carpet whenever you clean the grate. It is a thing one often skips, but sooty brooms and brushes make havoc of the carpet around the fender.

When carpets and rugs are brushed, and not cleaned by suction, it is advisable to keep brushes immaculately clean. Wash the carpet-brooms every week in tepid water, to which a little ammonia has been added. Dirty brooms merely spread the dirt, though they may remove surface dust. Use the suction cleaner *every* day. It preserves the life of the carpet, and keeps the colouring fast. The moment you see a spot on the carpet or rugs, rub it out with a mixture made from half methylated spirit and half ammonia. Don't swamp the place, but rub gently until the mark disappears. Neglected spots are much harder to clean than those which have been dealt with before the stain has set. Anyway, if you have left the marks too long, there is a clean patch left when you rub them out, which is hardly better than a dirty one.

Fading is not a problem in winter, but in summer it pays to draw the curtains when strong sun is about. It is perhaps not generally realised that sunlight rots, as well as fades, the carpet.

Shift stair carpet occasionally, so that the hard wear is better distributed. Move it upwards or downwards a few inches, to keep the bare patches at bay. Beware the worn castors which make holes in the carpet.

Very creditable repairs can be achieved by darning the bare patches on a rug with coloured wools. Use a carpet stitch, and colours which match the pattern.

Wallpapers and Linos

Watch the parts of the wallpaper that get the most wear. Prevent it if you can. Clean it off if it is there already.

In many rooms there is a dirty patch on the wallpaper just inside the door where people brush past. Try cleaning with art gum which you can buy from any artists' supply shop for a few pence.

Stale bread is a well-proved cleaner for soiled wallpaper, but if you can get it, the art gum is better.

If the decorators left a roll of the paper behind them—they often do—you can replace the dirty part with a panel of the new. Match the pattern carefully and it won't show.

Another measure is to hang a panel of embroidered silk or a charming damask in a narrow framing of wood where are the marks are. If your pattern is a quiet one, a strip of coloured hessian or crash linen boldly worked in bright coloured wools makes a very effective decoration and disguise for a worn place on the wall.

The same applies to that vulnerable patch between the settee or divan where men rest their heads upon the wall, invariably leaving a dark patch.

Linoleum is actually preserved as well as improved by polishing. A good wax polish feeds the linoleum and prevents it from cracking. Where cracks and worn parts are already showing a coating of Liquid Lino, which is made in a variety of colours, is a good covering. There is an old-fashioned trick of varnishing lino which might well be revived now. The effect is of a permanent gloss and the varnish protects it.

Just as with carpets it is sometimes possible to change the position of the linoleum by taking up a worn part and re-cutting it to replace a section that has been badly worn. The shabby piece can often be fitted again into a less conspicuous part.

Linen

Household linen may be impossible to replace later on so cosset the linen you have on hand.

There is little doubt that the laundry is the greatest menace to linen. Harsh chemicals reduce the lives of sheets and tablecloths, so if you can by any means get your laundry done at home now you are bound to score. Go over your stock in the linen cupboard regularly now, and take early steps to repair when the smallest signs of thinness begin to show. Tiny snags in tablecloths and bed linen can be neatly darned so that they scarcely show.

When putting clean sheets on the beds put the bottom of the sheets at the top sometimes. The greatest strain comes at that part of the sheet where the feet are constantly causing friction. Forget hemstitched tops for the time. Put tops to the bottom to give all sides a chance.

Old sheets that are beyond further use can be cut up, using the soundest parts to make new pillowcases. Large tablecloths can be cut down to make smaller ones, and old linen tablecloths make excellent table mats and table napkins.

Linen in constant use will wear out in the end, but you can put off the fatal day for a long while by keeping abreast of repairs and seeing to it that the fabric is preserved and not injured in the washing.

Upholstery and Curtains

Upholstered suites can be protected from wearing in the vulnerable parts by variations of the antimacassar. Slip tops for the back of the easy chairs where heads rest and for the arms save an immense amount of dirt and damage to fabric. If you happen to have any of the stuff with which the loose covers were made, neat slip-on arm covers and head rests can be easily fitted.

If the same material as the chair covering is not available, choose a plain fabric of a matching or toning colour with a similar texture to the original. These miniature slip covers are simple to make, and particularly simple to wash.

Tapestry and hair upholstery should be cleaned regularly with the suction cleaner. This draws out the dust and preserves the good colouring of the fabric. Spots and stains should be cleaned off regularly with a little carbon tetrachloride, which dissolves grease.

Furniture

Wash furniture regularly with a chamois cloth wrung out in a mixture of tepid water and vinegar. This cleans off grease and keeps the surface lustrous.

Hot marks on a polished surface can be removed by dabbing the spot with methylated spirit on a clean cloth following immediately with an application of linseed oil. Finish with polish. This may have to be repeated.

Fat or grease stains from gravy on the table top can be removed with carbon tetrachloride. Ink on wood or on leather upholstery will respond to treatment with tin chloride. Use a half-ounce to half pint of water. Apply directly by dropping from a piece of wood on to the spot. Remove the excess with blotting paper. Rinse with clean water and follow with polish.

Minor Repairs

Britannia & Eve (November 1944)

Furniture that has long been in store and some which has been exposed to bomb-blast will need many small repairs which can be done at home by the amateur with a few tools.

Drawers that will not run smoothly because of swelling caused by damp should be removed. If the sides of the drawer are examined, it will be found that the wood is shiny in those parts where the friction is hardest. Rub the top of the drawer sides very hard at these points with a coarse sand-paper. The very slight smoothing-off resulting from this will probably ease the trouble. Candle-grease or hard soap, rubbed on the parts before the drawer is replaced, will further improve matters.

Handles and drawer-knobs that have come off can be replaced with a little glue. If the hole into which the handle or drawer knobs fits has worn too large to fit the handle, this can be filled with a small quantity of plastic wood. Press the knob lightly smeared with glue, into the plastic wood before it hardens. Wipe the surplus paste away from the sides of the handle and leave to set.

A broken chair-leg is a little more tricky to repair. Place the two broken edges together with glue, and when this has dried attach a small piece of wood on the inside of the leg over the broken part with a screw at the top and bottom. This is the only way to give support to the break sufficient to take the weight of a person sitting in the chair.

Upholstered chair-seats that sag in the middle should be turned underside up and the canvas backing removed. The old webbing which holds the springs in place will be found, unless the springs themselves are broken, to be worn threadbare. Remove the old webbing and replace it, in the exact same way, with new. Draw the webbing very tightly across from one side of the chair-frame to the other, thus holding the springs in place. Replace the canvas and tack down firmly around the edges.

The absence of fathers, the possibility of homelessness, evacuation, and the stresses of wartime separation all impacted on the traditional family unit. Stereotypical expectations about gender roles meant that bad behaviour in children was often attributed to a disciplinarian father's absence. Mothers found themselves having to take on a paternal as well as maternal role, supplementing their own qualities with those of the father figure. Louisa Kay, writing in *Britannia & Eve* magazine in May 1943 advised that mothers who were parenting alone, 'must cultivate detachment and tolerance and an infinite discretion to add to those qualities of tenderness and toleration.'

As the war progressed, there was an increasing dislocation of living arrangements. Questions regarding the financial and legal obligations of homeowners and tenants in such uncertain times inevitably arose and demanded answers. Families might find themselves living with relations or sheltering displaced family members. Others ended up sharing homes with friends or neighbours out of necessity or for reasons of practical economy, and *Britannia & Eve* offered sage advice on how to nip inevitable tensions in the bud. Love, romance and marriage took on a more urgent and emotionally charged aspect, and with divorce cases in Britain increasing from 10,000 a year in 1938 to 25,000 in 1945, the problem of marital discord was a very real one, leading women's magazines to take on the role of marriage guidance counsellors. There was information for newlyweds from how to get married to how to negotiate living with in-laws, and mindful of the paranoia and worry that could arise from long separations, even prescriptive advice on what to write (and what not to write) in letters to sweethearts and husbands in order to maintain marital harmony.

War Law at Home

Britannia & Eve (February 1940)

The much abused D.O.R.A. of the last war was gradually evolved by practical experience; to-day an emergency code has sprung suddenly to life.

How does this sheaf of statues and regulations affect the women of wartime England in their everyday lives? Here are some of the questions which are asked today, and the legal answers.

Mrs. Green's husband used to earn £10 a week, but is now serving in the army as a private. She finds it impossible to pay the full rent of their house. What should she do?

Serving soldiers are not, as such, relieved from their liabilities in respect of rent, insurance premiums and so forth, although such protection was originally given to militiamen under the Military Training Act—now largely superseded by the National Service (Armed Forces) Act. Soldiers are thus at present in the same position as civilians.

Mrs. Green need not, however, be unduly worried, for the landlord cannot eject her or levy distress without first obtaining the leave of the Court.

Mrs. Green should have no difficulty in convincing the Court that it is entirely due to the war that the full rent cannot be paid. She will then be protected by the Courts (Emergency Powers) Act. If the judge is satisfied that the inability to pay the rent is due to circumstances "directly or indirectly attributable to the war," he has the power to refuse the landlord leave to re-enter on the property or to levy distress.

Alternatively, he may give leave subject to certain conditions. Mrs. Green should bear in mind that the debt is not extinguished, and although she may be allowed to remain in her house for the time being she should at once take steps to find a flat at a rent within her present means.

Mr. White entered into a hire-purchase agreement with X and Co. for his furniture. He has now lost his job owing to the war and is in arrears with the monthly instalments. Can X and Co. take possession of the furniture?

This case is covered by the same Act. X and Co. must obtain the permission of the Court before they retake the property.

If the sum owing is not more than £100 they must apply to the County Court, otherwise to the High Court. Mr. White will no doubt to convince the judge that it is because of the war, that he cannot pay the full instalments now, and he may be allowed to keep the furniture on certain conditions.

Shortly after war broke out, Miss Brown, who is buying a vacuum cleaner by instalments, was visited by an agent of the company who suggested that she might like to spread the sum owing over a longer period. She found the proposal inviting, but fortunately was wise enough to ask advice before signing the new agreement.

"Do not sign it," was the advice given to her. "If you do you will lose all protection which Parliament has given you under the Courts (Emergency Powers) Act.

If an agreement is signed after September 2, 1939, the company need not obtain the permission of the Court under that Act before retaking the cleaner. It is therefore much wiser to retain the original contract, although it is more onerous, and to keep up the payments to the best of your ability.

Mrs. Black lives in a flat. She is anxious to know whether the landlord can be made to provide an air raid shelter.

Under the Civil Defence Act the owner of a privately owned block of residential flats or maisonettes is bound to provide an air raid shelter if required to do so by more than one half of the occupants. This does not apply when the majority of the occupiers are provided free of charge by the Government with material for a shelter. If he provides a shelter the Landlord is allowed, in certain circumstances, to raise the rent.

These everyday examples show just a few of the ways in which Parliament has spoken in order to protect the individual and solve the problems caused by the war.

Miss Gray owes arrears of Income Tax for the years 1937 and 1938. She does not dispute that the money is due, and judgement has been signed against her. Owing to the war she now finds it doubly difficult to find the money: can the Crown force her pay without first obtaining the permission of the Court?

Yes. This point has recently been decided by a judge of the High Court. The Courts (Emergency Powers) Act, which gives protection to the debtor in other cases, does not bind the Crown. The Act contains no reference, either express or implied, to the Crown, and judgment can therefore be enforced without the permission of any Court.

Mrs. Jones is about to erect an air raid in her garden. Her lease comes to an end in nine months' time, and she wants to know whether she will be able to take the shelter with her when she moves to a new house. Will the shelters, like a greenhouse, conservatory or veranda, become a "landlord's fixture"?

This question has not yet been definitely decided, and Mrs. Jones will be wise if she first writes to her Landlord mentioning her intention to erect a shelter and asking to agree that, when the lease comes to an end, she may take the shelter with her. In the absence of such an agreement the question will be debatable. If the shelter can easily be removed it will probably be considered to be a tenant's fixture. If, on the other hand, it is embedded in earth and concrete, it is likely to be held to be a landlord's fixture, and Mrs. Jones will not be allowed to remove it.

Mrs. Smith has left her London house and is living in the country with her children. What should she do in order to avoid payment of rates on her evacuated house?

If the house remains furnished, rates must be paid, even though nobody lives there. Some local authorities, facing a serious decrease in revenue, may take the view that rates must be paid, even on an empty house, if the owner intends eventually to return to it; it seems, however, to be doubtful whether this convention will be legally upheld.

Harmony in One Flat

Britannia & Eve (February 1943)

People who call themselves realists are fond of saying that where you have two women running one home you will also have trouble.

This airy cliché is, thank goodness, disproved by the fact that everywhere women, finding themselves separated by the war from their men, are sharing homes with other women in the same plight and moreover, finding comfort and companionship and happiness therein.

Nobody seriously believes that the company of a woman is a hundred per cent substitute for that of a man's, but the women of sense making the best of it is a sound and profitable expedient.

The secret of happy housekeeping with another woman depends on three essentials. The first is selecting your partner intelligently; the second is anticipating and heading off possible sources of dispute; the third is a liberal and frequent application of tolerance and good humour.

Living happily with a woman who doesn't share your interests depends upon your mutual abilities to go your own ways without interference from each other. It does seem essential, however, to share each other's point of view on fundamental things.

Mutual money standards are still more important. It is easier to fall out of step with someone who has less or even more money than yourself than with somebody whose resources and tastes are in the same class as your own.

For instance, if one end of the partnership is used to housekeeping and entertaining on a lavish scale, while the other end models these things on strict economy, there are obvious points of discomfort, if not of actual disagreement.

It is true the more affluent partner may wish to wave these details aside. "I can afford it, I'll pay," she says, but to accept such an arrangement implies the need to accept an unequal distribution of authority. The soundest people are susceptible to the fallacy that he who pays the piper calls the tune.

Money is the biggest single cause of strife known to any kind of partnership. That is why a realistic understanding on the subject of payment down to the cost of the last package of salt is essential. A pool is probably the best solution for current housekeeping expenses. That is, each partner puts an agreed sum into the pool each week, and if there is any left over, it goes to the floating fund against possible deficiencies.

If you go shopping you take the money you have spent from the fund. If your partner goes shopping, or if either of you meet household expenses from your own purses, the money is refunded in the same way. Record your expenditure in a notebook. This is the tidy way. It leaves nothing to chance.

False pride about bringing money problems into the open and getting right down to tacks is fatal. If one partner nurses a grievance even for ten minutes because she thinks she is paying more than her share, there are the seeds of discontent well planted and ready to be fertilised by every trivial occurrence of the same kind.

A telephone can turn suddenly from a convenient instrument of communication into a perpetual bone of contention, unless there is a cast-iron system of payment which absolutely denies the possibility of either suspecting the other of secret, unpaid calls. These are molehills, perhaps, but they grow …

Furniture is another source of possible trouble.

In most such arrangements, some furniture belonging to each will be brought to the home. This probably means that both may have to live for the rest of the war with furnishing they don't particularly care for or wish to look after. We are all a bit susceptible to the notion that our taste in decoration is 100 per cent., but the true facts are that other people don't always agree, and why should they?

It is not important whether or not you like your partner's taste in furnishing. What *is* worth considering is the fact that the presence of personal possessions in the home is to each person a great source of contentment, so put up with that.

One of the partners may have to get used to a narrow single bed. Few flats are big enough to allow a double bed for each.

A single divan in the sitting-room, if you have one, solves the sleeping problem for one.

The accommodation of clothes and toilet necessities wants a little more thought. In one case the problem was met by utilising the deep sitting-room cupboard. A long strip of glass fixed inside the cupboard-door serves for a dressing mirror. Shelves running across were cut to run around three sides, leaving space in the centre for a hanging-rail.

Shelves on one side now hold toilet articles, those on the other take hats, shoes, and so on.

This way the cupboard covers the purposes of wardrobe, dressing-table and chest of drawers, and leaves the sitting-room unblemished by bedroom fittings.

It goes without saying that the harmony of the house will be improved if both have their own tasks, and if these are allotted to conform as far as possible with mutual talents and tastes. If one is a good cook (which probably means that she enjoys cooking), and the other has a sharp nose for shopping, then each should do the work she likes best without too much interference from the other. As to the tasks that both dislike, nothing will suffice but a strictly fifty-fifty share-out and no quitting.

Entertaining friends and husbands depends on generosity and a candid working understanding.

Privacy to entertain personal friends and relatives without responsibility to the other partner is essential, and a special understanding about husbands on leave should be reached at the start.

Short reunions cannot be expected to stand the intrusion of a third party. Their joy depends upon two being alone, tucked between four walls, free to talk and to reconstruct the old happy home atmosphere alone. Both women, in turn, will benefit from a candid and generous understanding that on leaves the privacy of the reunited must be respected.

The whole philosophy of sharing a home is expressed in the simple term "toleration." Bear in mind that the privilege of companionship does not confer the additional privilege upon either party of changing that person's habits and mannerisms in the smallest degree. If either finds that the established ways of the other are disagreeable to the extent of being important at all, then the only inference to be drawn is that the partnership should never have been started anyway.

Wedding in a Hurry

Britannia & Eve (May 1944)

Short leaves, dynamic meetings of girl and boy which ripen quickly into marriage are making parsons and registrars very busy people. Marriages in haste are taking place everywhere and trailing their problems in their wake.

Getting married has been somewhat simplified for Service people by sympathetic authorities who, appreciating the difficulties, have dispensed, in certain instances, with the more tedious formalities.

Members of the Forces can, for instance, be married by special license at a register office within forty-eight hours of its issue. It costs £2 14s. 7d., whereas a similar licence for a church ceremony costs £2 5s. 6d. with the addition of the vicar's fee which varies, but averages a guinea.

One of the parties concerned must have been domiciled in the district where the marriage is to be performed, for fifteen days. This means that if the bridegroom is stationed at, say, Birmingham, and the bride lives at, say, Norwich, they can only be married by special licence at either one of those two places. Otherwise the fifteen days' residence must be established elsewhere.

Two witnesses are required at a marriage, but their identity is unimportant. Friends or strangers will do—even the lady who scrubs the register office will suffice if someone lets you down.

Best men and bridesmaids are charming conventions, but they make no difference whatever to the legality of the marriage rites so long as two other witnesses are available.

When the groom is in uniform, the choice of a bridal outfit is influenced only by personal taste and the immediate coupon situation. At quiet weddings these days, most sensible brides choose an outfit which renders the most practical service after the day with, perhaps, a certain amount of relaxation from austerity in the choice of a hat. A frivolous hat never fails to impart festivity to the wearer.

Problem number one on the bride's horizon, in these days of meetings and hasty marriages away from the usual background of home and parental interception, is Meeting His People For The First Time.

Meeting the relations of the man you are going to marry is an ordeal at all times. Meeting them when your marriage has, as it were, been sprung on them, enhances these points and calls for considerable poise at a time when poise is somewhat severely strained.

Brides about to endure the parental once-over should remember that to be too critical is to invite criticism in return. The mother of the man you're about to marry is only human and motherly in wishing the best for her son. By sympathizing with her alarms, one quickly dispels them unless she is an impossible person. Mothers-in-law, apart from the music-hall stage variety, are not often like this.

Don't expect to lean upon your new husband too heavily in this ordeal. Men are understandably bewildered at this stage of relations between wife and mother by what they are pleased to regard as feminine difficulties. In any case the poor man is anxious to please both of you which is never easy and frequently impossible.

Starting a home from scratch just now is frequently not even feasible, but luckier brides can at least lay the foundations for a later start, by planning and ordering certain things which may be a long time materializing.

A new Board of Trade order makes permits for Utility furniture available to all couples married since the war.

The permits are issued at local Fuel Control Centres and the purchase can be made wherever the furniture is available. For the moment no promises are made as to the available quantities, but the production situation is improving rapidly.

Problem number one on the bride's horizon is Meeting His People For The First Time

Two witnesses are required—even the lady who scrubs the register office will suffice, if someone lets you down

Passed by the Censor

Britannia & Eve (October 1942)

When you write to a man who is far from home there are several very important things to keep in mind.

First of these, if he happens to be your husband or somebody with serious plans for filling that office, is that your letters are probably the most important things in his life. That leaves you with a big responsibility to sustain, and means that you can't sit down and glibly dash off the first things that come into your head.

The next is that the things you can get away with in personal contact are apt to become a menace when written down. There is a mysterious something about the written word that is potentially dangerous. A mere inflection of the voice when you speak, the addition of a smile, will render even the riskiest remark innocuous, whereas the most innocent comment in writing and without the aid of these palliatives becomes an arsenal of dangerous and explosive implication.

Everybody knows that the domestic quarrel is a normal and even a healthy manifestation of the married state. It comes and it goes. You call your husband names and threaten to leave him and he replies in kind. Ten minutes later he has suggested a movie and you have started knitting that new pair of socks you promised him. But you can't quarrel like that through the post.

Those very things that you have often said so light-heartedly in his presence and which he has accepted with the same spirit have a new and more menacing implication in black and white.

To conduct a safe correspondence with a man who is far away you have first of all to put yourself in his shoes.

Your man wants news of home, but primarily he wants to be reminded of the home he knew and loved.

Not of some strange place that home has become since he left it. The chances are fifty to one that he will recoil from the news of fundamental changes. If your letters convey to him that you have changed your outlook and your mode of life so liberally since he went that he begins to doubt if he will fit in at all when the time comes for his return, then the pleasure of news from home is tempered with anxiety.

Assurances of your happiness and well-being are absolutely essential to a man's peace of mind if he loves you, but when these assurances are so emphatic that he begins to wonder if you are not getting along too swimmingly without him then the inevitable fat begins to splutter in the fire.

Put yourself in the place of a man who has been sweltering for months under German shell fire in the Libyan desert, whose wife or fiancée writes him three pages of eulogy upon the compensations of working in a war factory where there is a super social club at which she can attend a dance three times a week. It doesn't want much imagination to understand that the effects of dust and heat and thirst and danger and the rest of it are in no sense relieved by the knowledge that your woman is at home doing the rhumba in the arms of some fellow who, by a mere freak of fortune, is spared from serving his country in a place where there are no girls but only a pitiless sun.

There are few serving men to-day who are afraid of Germans, but the toughest of them is apt to come unpinned before the fear, which frequently exists without the smallest calculable basis of reason, that his influence with the woman he loves is declining.

It is a deadly insidious torture. It is an anxiety frequently established and nourished by careless letter-writing. Women have a lot to answer for.

Don't tell him the big news of your daily life just because it is big. Weigh the consequences of everything you say. In charity withhold those things which may puzzle, annoy or worry him. On the other hand don't obviously withhold things.

CHAPTER 2
MAKE DO AND MEND

News and advice on fashion and clothing had formed the basis of mainstream women's magazines since their first appearance in the 19th century. The war years were no exception, but the introduction of clothes rationing in June 1941 meant fashion journalism was forced to take a new direction. Women were advised to change their thinking from 'What can I have new for autumn?' to 'Can I do without?'. For many, clothes rationing was one of the most dismal aspects of wartime living. They were told by the President of the Board of Trade, 'When you feel tired of your old clothes, remember that by making them do you are contributing some part of an aeroplane, a gun or tank,' but it must have felt difficult to make the connection when faced with such a stringent cutbacks. Posters, advertisements and leaflets introducing the character 'Mrs Sew-and-Sew' in 1943, advised women to 'make do and mend' but there was more to wartime dressing than perpetually darning worn clothes.

Britannia & Eve explained that the canny fashionista should do some long-term planning and use coupons to buy quality garments that would last. Many pages were devoted to suggesting items that when combined together, or with existing garments would form a hard-working capsule wardrobe. Adapting, rather than continually mending pre-war clothes, with their more generous fabric content was another way to eke out clothes. Imagination and ingenuity were encouraged. The nation's women were not found wanting in this department, and magazines provided inspiration with drawings of current fashions and specific make-do-and-mend projects. Old slips became evening boleros, men's jackets shrunk down into children's coats, fashionable bishop sleeves were fashioned out of dirndl skirts, and spare strips of fabric could be used for frills and embellishments. Even the Queen admitted that she had dabbled in some re-styling by having, 'an old hat turned inside out, remade, and it looked like new.'

Dress

By Jean Burnup (Editor Women's Department)

Britannia & Eve (September 1942)

The clothes situation, pared down to the bone, seems to have brought out the master mind in all of us.

In fifteen short months, with the adaptability that has characterised all their activities in these changing times, women have dropped the free-and-easy, buy-on-sight habits of a lifetime and have acquired the more valuable habit of knowing what not to buy.

We have learned to take the long view about clothes, and not to be circumscribed by seasons. We exploit interchangeability to its limit, we plan wardrobes whose future is just as important as their present.

And, as dress restrictions in detail, styling and ornamentation are themselves giving clothes a new, clear-cut tang, buying restrictions are shaping new standards of taste for women everywhere.

Since the Government ask you, as man to man, to buy only what you really need, it follows that the luxurious woman is as much out of the current picture as neon lighting.

In ye olde days, being in the fashion was unessential. What mattered was that your clothes became you and expressed your individuality. That is out. To-day you have to be in the fashion and let your individuality go and play dormouse till the war is over.

And the fashion is a well-groomed, slick simplicity for every day and all day, with occasional excursions into glamour for celebrations that happen along. Even though this simplicity tends to be almost as uniform as a uniform itself, women are gaining, if anything, in appearance.

The questions "Can I do without it?" is far more vital to-day than the question "What can I have new for autumn?" which used to engross us at this time of the year.

So the basic wardrobe, drawn in the first panel, admittedly sparse, is workable for an average woman. Naturally, you could manage easier with more, but you could support life, without discomfort, on less. The point is that everything you possess, every new purchase, must work hard for its keep. Passenger clothes are out for the duration.

The suit, with shirts and sweaters, is, of course the great all-year-round stand-by. Women not at their best in a strictly-tailored suit should consider a short-sleeved dress and matching jacket. It is elegant, supremely comfortable and alive with interchangeable potentialities. It gives you an extra light-weight woollen frock.

AVERAGE / BASIC WARDROBE   MAJOR BUYS

WINTER COAT   SUIT   NEW COAT   OR   JACKET DRESS

2 SWEATERS   2 SHIRTS   CARDIGAN HANDKNIT   DRESSY BLOUSE   ODD SKIRT   SUMMER COAT AND   ODD SKIRT

WOOL DRESS   SILK DRESS   HEATWAVE DRESS   2 DRESSES ONE WOOL ONE SILK

HOUSE COAT-DRESSING GOWN   SLIP   3 NIGHTDRESSES   SUIT   OR   3 NIGHTIES

3 CAMIKNICKERS   2 SETS OF WOOLLIES   2 BELTS   2 BRAS OR CORSELETTES   3 CAMIKNICKERS AND 1 SLIP

Bourle jacket dress, made in several good colours, including black, with interesting gathering and seaming detail at yoke. (Dickins and Jones. £15 11s. 3d.

(Top) Beige and brown check suit, good detail on jacket pocket, three knife pleats in front, one back of skirt. Bourne and Hollingsworth, £9 19s. 6d.

36

5 PRS OF SHOES   6 PRS OF STOCKINGS   3 PRS OF WOOLLEN UNDIES

SPARE PARTS

SCARVES

SUMMER OR FABRIC GLOVES

HANKERCHIEFS

RAINCOAT

ANKLE SOCKS

LINNEN OR ORDINARY SLACKS

HOTWEATHER DRESS

OVERALL

BED JACKET

KNITTING WOOL

DRESSING GOWN

YEARLY MUSTS

Six Pairs Stockings

One Pair Shoes

Two Belts and Brassieres or Corselettes

One Pair Gloves

If your clothes reserves have spent themselves and you now have to be a one-silk-dress woman, let the dress be plain, not patterned. Then it is mobile all year round. A flower-dotted crepe hasn't much appeal at Christmas.

Each year, your musts (see yearly musts list) will take up about 25 coupons. That leaves 25. That means one major buy in the year. That means a margin of seven or eight coupons over for spare parts (see panel 3), which you will buy only according to your special activities and not your desires.

Remember that if you think you need a new coat this year, but know you are out of woollen underwear, the coat will have to be forsworn, and the major buy will have to be the unexciting underwear.

But perhaps you have woollen fingers and can knit your own and save a few coupons. We shall print a good design next month.

"Dress: 2 into 1, 1 into 2"

By Jean Burnup

Britannia & Eve (October 1941)

The London shops have never shown better merchandise. Credit rationing, which makes it obligatory for clothes to be made of fabrics and designs that will endure. (1) This coat is a Jaeger and its cut, tailoring and fabric carry all that that name implies. (Details: adroit bodice pleats narrowing to the waist, vertical slit pockets, a full skirt.) In mohair and woollen mixture, scarlet and all pastels, it costs eleven guineas. (2) This black woollen dress from Fenwick uses self-ruching, with fine effect, on pockets and the high-or-low collar. Also in tan, turquoise, lacquer-red. £7 17s. 6d. (3) A tailored woollen suit featuring padded seaming on pockets and across the back yoke. The skirt has pleats stitched to thighs, either side. 11 guineas, in brown or black, from Dickins and Jones. (4) The front of this black bouclét coat is as intriguing as the back, with its high revers, double breasting, black velvet collar and large patch pockets. Double seams down the back bodice become pleats below the shaped waist, are stitched to mid-skirt, then kick out. £9 19s. 6d., from Fenwick. (5) Pure woollen suit (Jaeger again), the plain jacket trimmed with stitching and slit hip pockets, the hulabuloo check skirt flaring slightly, on the bias. Blue jacket, with blue, cherry-pink and red skirt, or gold jacket with a gold, red and green skirt. 13 guineas.

1 into 2

(1) This tartan taffeta little-woman dinner dress, circa 1937, is still as good as gold, but has outgrown its place in your heart. Cut it off about five inches below the waist

and turn the top into the short-sleeved basqued jumper (2). This practically makes itself. The yards and yards left in the skirt are enough to make the cute little waisted afternoon dress (3).

These full, deep-belted skirted dresses (4) were everywhere before the war. If you are lucky enough to possess one, take it to pieces, add some unrationed matching lace, two yards of contrast crepe (or the best of an old slip or nightdress), and you have two frocks. Make a flat cross-over bodies with panels extending to the hem (5). Treat the back the same. Fill in the four inverted V's of the skirt with lace, fill in the bodice sides with lace. Use the old sleeves, shortened. You will find you have only scratched the surface of your fabric, and that there is plenty left to make the back, sides and sleeves of the apron-fronted dress (6).

2 into 1

A light woollen jacket and skirt (7) is soon turned into an elegant woollen frock (8). Cut the jacket off at waist and join to the skirt. Remove the pockets. Cut the sleeves off as shown, and gather them slightly into the bend of the elbow. Cut along the top of the skirt's inverted pleat and arrange the fullness into a gathered panel. Trim with tasselled braid.

Tired housecoat (9) and nightdress long in the tooth (10) can be successfully combined thus. Cut three strips gradually widening to the hem from the skirt of the housecoat and hoard them safely for some future renovation. Fill with strips cut from the nightdress and you have a new dinner dress (11). We have not drawn it so, but you could, if you are the fluffy sort, wear a ruffle (from the nightdress) round the throat and down the bodice front.

New Clothes from Old Discards

Britannia & Eve (May 1942)

Make no mistake about it, fifteen coupons less off your quota is quite a slice. Two courses are open to you. The first is to shrug your shoulders and say: "So what? Even if I had the coupons and the money, the Government don't want me to spend unnecessary money, because they want me to save labour and material. Might as well give in and settle down to a skirt-and-sweater sort of existence—not really drab, but just not bothering."

That's the easy way, and nobody is going to blame you for taking it. The trouble is that, once you start not bothering, you are inclined to slide. So that, pretty soon, grease spots on your coat lapel, turned-over heels and threadbare elbows don't bother you either. It is the same attitude of mind as that of the housewife who uses short rations as an excuse for monotonous and slovenly cooking. There is, as yet, no excuse for it.

The other course is to brace your shoulders and say: "True, I am helping my country when I don't buy unnecessary new clothes. But I am just being defeatist if I turn myself into a drab dowd. So, if it's all the same to everyone, while I am still in civil life, I am going to take a lot of trouble to look as nice as possible under existing circumstances. This means spending quite a bit of my shortened spare time on upkeeping my existing clothes. I have to be ingenious and imaginative about any future buys. I'll have to be ruthless about editing inessentials even if they have an uplift value, and sometimes I'll have to cut out essentials. I'll give the same care and attention to the job of altering old clothes as I once gave to selecting new ones. That is the course that, in these difficult days, is going to help me most, and, I hope, help those around me."

If you feel that way then, here is a bunch of change-over ideas for warm-weather and celebration clothes. You may be able to adapt some of them to your own requirements. If the amendments sound too professional, take them along—but quickly, for they are busy and short-handed—to those big stores which have this kind of service. You will find, too, that many formerly ritzy dressmakers are not too proud, these days, to turn their fine hands to alterations.

1. A plain dress and frock in grey woollen is given new heart with a trimming of plum and white spotted woollen. If you haven't this sort of stuff by you, it will take about three-eighths of a yard. The dress pocket is made from what is left after lopping off the coat sleeves to make them the new three-quarter length.
2. For this outfit you need an old summer print and the silk slip of an old evening dress for the bolero, sash and hem band. Cut away some of the skirt fullness, and you have plenty of material for the gloves.
3. This is a simpler job made out of a plain, not particularly interesting dark woollen frock, buttoning down front. Cut strips away from either side of the front, remove collar, join the front with bands and wear over a bright silk shirt-vest.

4. This little black frock has been seen around for over three years. Who is going to recognise it with the fullness gone from the skirt and turned into flouncy trimming?

5. This elegant dinner outfit calls for two discards. An old decollete evening dress—most of us have one eating its head off in our wardrobe—and an outgrown bright woollen frock that has perhaps shrunk in cleaning, or lost its appeal. Well, the frock makes the sweater. Use it all, recklessly—it's worth it. Cut the evening dress off at the waist, and make your skirt. Trim your sweater with fringe to match the skirt. I visualise a stunning combination in cyclamen and cornflower blue.

6. Most of us have had a print dress with a draped bodice, a corselet waist, and a full skirt. All its old friends would pass it by in the new guise of a slim skirt, and a cute little basque (made from the skirt's fullness).

7. A very full dirndl dress with a corselet waist comes out as fresh as a paint with bishop sleeves (from what you cut away of the skirt) and coloured braiding trim.

8. The only excuse for tampering with a plain, long-sleeves, sleek black dinner-frock is that you are really bored with it. If and when that happens, cut off the top and shape the corsage. Fill in with bishop sleeves and a yoke of unrationed net or lace.

Beg Borrow or Steal

By Vere Denning

Britannia & Eve (November 1940)

Dressing well is a matter of ingenuity these days. We're spending less. Many of us are living out of reach of the shops, or our war work doesn't leave us time for a good old-fashioned shopping jag. And although we have been extraordinarily lucky in the way our little luxuries are still allowed us, there is a certain drying-up of supplies, naturally, and making-do with a flourish becomes a virtue.

It's remarkable how many other people's belongings can be requisitioned once you put your mind to it, in order to keep looking smart and the very opposite gone to pieces. I'm not suggesting—heaven forbid—a raid on your sister-in-law's silk stockings or your bridesmaid's furs. But take a look at shops which you have always walked past, bored, and see if there isn't something there which you can press into your own service.

You want a new bag? Leather is expensive, you must have something which will last and you've always been a snob about handbags. No need for a moment's worry, here. Find an old-fashioned saddler's shop. There is one in even the most stuck-in-the-mud reception area. Poke about until you find one of the cash bags which he probably makes for the local milkman. They are made of the toughest brown calf, fastening with a flap. They have a long strap which you can sling over your shoulder, just like the bags Schiaparelli charge five guineas for. This one will set you back less than 7s. 6d. and look wonderful with your country clothes and your chunky flat-heeled shoes.

In the same shop, or in almost any trunk shop, you should be able to find yourself a very good-looking pigskin belt with a plain, square, covered buckle. In a leather shop they sell them for men for about 5s. You can easily have one shortened to fit you.

Hats are a problem this winter. You have one really good one which you keep for special occasions, but what about something to wear when you want to do the shopping and can't bear the sight of another turban or hood? Here the answer is in any boys' outfitters.

Little boys wear grey flannel hats (they look like felt, don't be alarmed) which are enormously becoming if you put on a better ribbon and wear them smack on the back of your head, like an American college girl. You can but these either stitched or plain for less than five shillings a go.

While you are in the shop, take a look at some boys' shoes known as the Cambridge shape. They have high fronts and gussets of elastic. William wears them as house shoes, but what is to stop you from wearing them instead of those infinitely more expensive flat-heeled elastic-sided American shoes which are in any case rather difficult to get now? I admit that you can't do this trick if you have a very sophisticated foot fitting, but it's worth trying, considering the prices start at 8s. 11d.

On the way out, you might like to get a snake-buckle belt. They are fun for wearing with sweaters, and you can find masses of good colour combinations.

Nurses' outfitters yield one brain-wave. They have the prettiest ruched cuffs which are used for keeping up rolled-up sleeves. There's nothing to stop you from wearing them to freshen up a dark short-sleeved dress, but be sure to buy them in organdie; the lawn kind are too heavy to be smart.

Several men's shops are selling knee-high woollen socks in the gayest reds, yellows and blues. They stay up by themselves because of special elasticised tops, and they cost something like five shillings. You could wear these over hopelessly laddered stockings. They are newer than ankle socks for the country.

And now for a few pretty bits which aren't essentials, but can do a lot to raise your spirits as you can put on a suit you wish you need never see again. Rake junk shops for oddments you can turn into lapel clips. Don't go to antique-shops or second-hand jewellers—they are far too obvious and expensive. Try, instead, grubby little shops in back streets, and those mysterious places which buy old silver and gold.

For a couple of shillings you may find a locket which you can have made into an identity disc; or a Victorian vinaigrette which will look like a million-dollar clip when you pin it to your suit. You might even like to pack it with smelling salts for use in an emergency.

Decanter labels, in silver or coloured enamel, are another amusing idea for a clip. Find two or three pretty ones and fasten them on with a carefully-tied flat-bow in petersham ribbon.

And to carry all your findings and stealings home, beg or borrow a charwoman's coloured string bag. There's no shopping-bag on earth to touch it. It holds the most improbable quantities, yet collapses flat enough to tuck into a handbag when empty.

Good garment care was fundamental to prolonging the life of a woman's wardrobe, and it involved a considerable investment of time. 'Mending and repairing has not figured over much in the average woman's accomplishments lately', admitted *Britannia & Eve* in a feature devoted to giving a detailed run-down of the rudiments of patching and darning. Government-sponsored classes in department stores, schools and village halls were all part of a national drive to turn women into resourceful seamstresses. With so many women on their feet all day, the lifespan of shoes could be extended by regular cleaning and repairs, as well as soles reinforced by Phillips stick-a-soles. Some suggestions, such as home dry-cleaning, lining men's trouser pockets with chamois leather or stitching a leather strip into turn-ups to prevent wear, seem painstaking beyond words, but are proof of how important it was to preserve clothing in the face of drastic shortages.

We're On The Mend...

Britannia & Eve (August 1941)

A good many of us must accept the fact that whatever we might teach our grandmothers it would not be anything about patching and darning. Mending and repairing has not figured over much in the average woman's list of accomplishments lately, but the time has come to change all that and to be on the mend or endure a lingering shabbiness.

Mending is quite a fascinating study. A neat repair is a satisfying thing and can increase the life of clothes and house linen by a long time.

You need patience rather than skill to do good repairs. It is what some people call fiddling work, but it isn't difficult if you follow the rules.

One of the first essentials is to use the right implements and the right mending materials. One is apt to be careless about the size of a needle or the exact colour of a thread, but you can be assured that these are the small things which wreck your chances of achieving an invisible repair.

Use a long, thin needle for most darning work. Sometimes it is necessary in wool darning to use a slightly heavier one because the mending wool is heavy, but generally speaking, unsightly darns are due to thread too heavy for the background fabric and needles too clumsy.

Before repairing stockings choose the thread carefully. Keep a mending basket well stocked with mending threads of various colours and weights. Select one for the job which is neither too heavy for the stocking nor too delicate to cover the hole successfully.

When you sew a patch use a fine needle to ensure tiny invisible stitches. Have plenty of needles and several pairs of scissors of varying sizes.

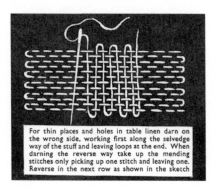

For thin places and holes in table linen darn on the wrong side, working first along the selvedge way of the stuff and leaving loops at the end. When darning the reverse way take up the mending stitches only picking up one stitch and leaving one. Reverse in the next row as shown in the sketch

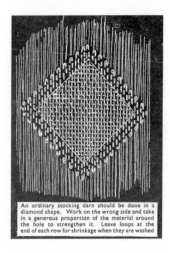

An ordinary stocking darn should be done in a diamond shape. Work on the wrong side and take in a generous proportion of the material around the hole to strengthen it. Leave loops at the end of each row for shrinkage when they are washed

Always cut away the ragged edges of a hole before darning. Start the repair stitches well outwards on either side of the hole so that its weak sides are reinforced. Leave loops at each end when pulling through the thread to allow for shrinkage in the wash.

When dealing with the formidable kind of hole which afflicts children's stockings, try placing a piece of coarse net behind the hole and darn through it. This gives you more control and thoroughly strengthens the repair.

Darn on the wrong side and work in a diamond shape for preference.

Protective darning should be done wherever there is thinness. Darn over the place with a thin thread of matching colour. Again the stitches should be taken on the wrong side of the garment.

In nearly all wool materials it is best to unpick the lining of the garment and to unravel pieces of thread sufficient to darn over the hole. This takes a little time, but it is the only way to get a truly invisible repair.

When darning or patching, take particular care to lay the patch or take the darning stitches with the weave of the material. Unless you do this the repair will never be flat and neat. If the garment is cut on the cross, lay your patch on the cross too, and if the material is figured be meticulous in matching the pattern at the edges of the patch.

Holes in tweed or other woollens are generally best handled by tacking a patch onto the back of the hole and darning it over very neatly on the right side with ravellings taken from the hem.

To make a patch in thinner materials, go to work like this:—

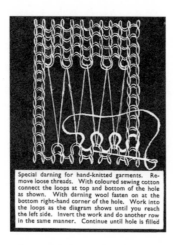

Special darning for hand-knitted garments. Remove loose threads. With coloured sewing cotton connect the loops at top and bottom of the hole as shown. With darning wool fasten on at the bottom right-hand corner of the hole. Work into the loops as the diagram shows until you reach the left side. Invert the work and do another row in the same manner. Continue until hole is filled

First cut the patch, making it large enough to come well outside the edges of the hole, leaving enough for a small turning at the edges.

Turn down a narrow hem all around the patch on the right side. Press it; place the patch on the wrong side of the garment with the turnings inwards. Be sure to get the patch running with the weave of the garment. Tack it down, taking special care to get the corners flat and neat. Now, using the smallest stitches, hem it all round.

Take out tacking threads when this is done and turn the garment over to the right side. Cut the hole diagonally to within a small space of each corner. Turn in the four edges, taking care to get the corners as flat as possible. Tack down the edges and oversew.

Take out the tacking threads and press the patch.

Blankets which have developed thin patches should be darned over with wool, and where a definite hole has appeared a patch of flannel should be applied.

When the edges of blankets become frayed, trim these off and either bind with ribbon or blanket stitch with coloured wool.

If you own a sewing machine you can do the most skilful repairs and very quickly at that with the darning attachment which is obtainable for about six shillings.

No special skill is required to operate the attachment but special lessons are given free at Singers' sewing machine agents.

Darns in both wool and cotton garments and also in household linens can be done on the machine both rapidly and neatly.

Care for Clothes

By Vere Denning

Britannia & Eve (February 1940)

I have no quarrel with dry cleaners. Mine are excellent, and before Sir John Simon played such an absorbing part in my life, my weekly bundle of clothes to clean and press must have paid most of their rent.

Now—alas for their profits but goody-goody for my budget—I have learned to be my own valet. Gather round and I'll tell you how you can still look just out of the band-box, though your suit is threatening to leave you and live on its Old Age Pension.

First, don't stint on equipment. A lumpy blanket on a corner of the kitchen table will not make you the wizard with the smoothing-iron which your tightened purse-strings insists you must be.

A properly-covered ironing-board is essential, not too wide for your skirts to be slipped easily round it. Sleeve boards always seem to be designed for ironing elephant's clothes. I find a padded rolling-pin far more useful. If you can run to an automatically heat-controlled iron, it makes the job absolute bliss, but a 7s. 6d. electric iron isn't to be despised, and the miniature travelling iron which you have popped away somewhere comes in very useful for tricky bits of frilling, as well as for negotiating puff sleeves, your own or the children's.

A small sponge is a help (3d. from a chemist) and you must have an adequate cloth for pressing, which won't leave bits of fluff behind on dark materials.

Since rayon has crept into most fabrics these days, never try to press a blouse or dress without first covering it with your evenly damp cloth. The result, if you ignore this heart-felt warning, will be a shiny patch which nothing will remove. With a damp cloth you can also unseat that skirt which has developed a pocket at the back for you to sit in. Slip the skirt over the board, with the baggy side facing you but wrong side out. Cover it with a very damp cloth and press with a hot iron until you have shrunk the material back to its original shape. Do this often and you won't have to work so hard over the job.

Now we come to men's suits. Give your husband fair warning that you intend to go through his pockets. Turn each pocket inside out and brush thoroughly; turn down the turn-ups of the trousers and clear out the road sweepings that have found a home there. Sew on any buttons that need it, and do the job thoroughly with proper linen thread, not 40 cotton, if they are buttons which take any strain.

If your husband's pockets develop money-losing holes, make new ones of thin chamois leather, and remind him to get his tailor to put this type in next time he buys a new suit. Good tailors will also stitch a strip of leather inside the back heel of each trouser leg, to prevent the turn-up from cutting through.

If any trousers have not been fitted with this, be sure to stitch a strip in yourself before any further damage is done.

On a loved but disreputable gardening jacket, out at elbows and frayed at the cuffs, you can fix patches of brown or chamois leather. I don't advise this as a beautiful surprise, though—have a word with the owner about it first.

When pressing a suit, always use a damp cloth, and take special care to get the crumples out of the sleeves. Follow the old trouser creases as though they were your mother's precepts, a misplaced crease is a major tragedy.

If you don't seem very good at this part of the job, buy an electric trouser-pressing gadget which is just whisked down each leg while the trousers are on. This costs 12s. 6d., and many a business man and woman has achieved a terrific reputation for grooming by secreting one in the office drawer, for it is equally good for pleated skirts.

To remove a generally shiny look, sponge, not too lavishly, with a weak solution of ammonia and water, then press under a dry cloth.

If the seat is very shiny, rub with a cut potato. Then cover with a damp cloth and press with a series of bangs. After each bang, lift up the cloth and tease the pile of the fabric with a stiff brush while it is still steaming.

Men's hats, like your own, need a rub over inside every week with a spirit cleaner to remove brilliantine from his, powder from yours. They both respond unbelievably by being held in the steam of a boiling kettle, then brushed.

If his hats get ruined by hair oil, you might try hiding a band of clean blotting paper behind the inside band, changing it often and hoping you won't be discovered.

Most of the stains which used to make you send clothes to the cleaner in the old days can be removed with a good spirit cleaner such as Thawpit.

Keep a bottle in your bedroom, and use it to whisk off that infuriating powder mark which spoils the neckline of your black dresses, that grease mark at the back of the neck. The smell disappears in a moment, and even on a light fabric there is no danger of a ring if you blow furiously on the spot while rubbing it with the cleaner.

Both your husband's shoes and your own will last longer, and keep the rain out better, if they are long-soled when they need it. The cost is not much more than the half-soling most people have, but the difference in comfort is immense, and you don't have that depressed feeling of wearing obviously soled shoes.

Did you know that very fine glasspaper can be used to restore the first shiny patches on suède shoes? And did you know that hopelessly shiny suède can be transformed into glossy new kid?

Get a tube of good shoe cream, the white kind, such as Meltonian. Apply it with a clean soft cloth all over the shoes, working it well in and doing only a small patch at a time. A pair of shoes ought to take you an hour and it doesn't do to hurry the job. Start with the heels, and work away until you have polished the suède surface to a smooth shining kid.

Every one will think you have some new kid shoes, but you won't be able to resist telling them the truth—you will be feeling so disgustingly smug about this brilliant wartime economy.

Dry Clean at Home

Britannia & Eve (October 1943)

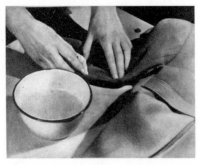

Before using any cleaning agent on a dirty or spotted garment, always try cleaning first with plain cold water. Even if this is not entirely successful, it always helps to loosen the stain before applying a solvent

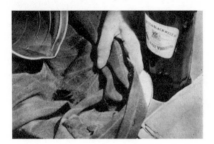

Woollen garments stained with perspiration should be sponged with a mixture of warm water and vinegar in the proportion of one tablespoonful to the pint. Be careful not to saturate the material

Magnesia will absorb grease spots from most woolly materials. Sprinkle it on the spot, rub it in gently, then roll up the garment and leave it over-night. Next day brush out with a soft-bristle brush

Fur gloves can be cleaned successfully with powdered magnesia. Rub the preparation into the skin with the tips of the fingers, leave it for a few hours, and then shake vigorously to remove surplus powder

Splashes of iodine can be removed with bicarbonate of soda dissolved in a little warm water. Apply on a cloth and rub gently. Repeat the treatment if necessary

Velvet and velveteen materials which have spotted should be sprinkled with powdered pipe-clay. Leave for an hour or two and then brush gently out

Repair Your Own Fur Coat

Britannia & Eve (October 1944)

Any day now I shall take a walk around the big stores and look at the fur coats. This is partly to indulge a purely romantic illusion that I might buy one, partly self discipline ; a measure, in fact, to convince myself that my old fur coat is still a better proposition than any of those.

After this, I shall go home and try to make it come true.

If I had thought of it three months ago I could have turned the whole business over to a furrier, but I omitted to do this, so the alternative to wearing a once-good coat that now looks like a starving cat just in out of the rain is to do it myself.

Fur renovating by home process does work out. Given enough time and thoroughness and the right cleaning materials, it is not so formidable as it may seem.

First step is to take out the lining and wash it. This has to be done carefully in warm soapy water so that the fabric does not shrink and land you with a lining several inches too small for the coat.

If the lining has worn threadbare at the turnings, as it frequently does, it can be strengthened by machining bias binding along the worn edges before replacing it. If the coupon situation permits, buy new material and cut a new lining, with the old one as a pattern.

Splits in the coat often prove to be in the joins between the skins. When the lining is removed and the coat turned on the wrong side, these and other weak places can be easily seen.

Use a glover's needle to sew these together. Lay the parted edges of the skin together and oversew them neatly with a thin strong thread.

Cuffs that are worn down to the skin at the edges can sometimes be turned up just sufficient to hide the threadbare part without making the sleeves too short. If the coat is cut on full lines the front edges can also be turned in a fraction with the same result.

To clean the fur and restore its lustre, hang the coat out in the sun and beat it thoroughly with a thin cane to remove the dust which clings within the fur.

Now moisten some bran with hot water—dry powdered magnesia is good too if you can get it. Rub gently all over the surface of the fur and leave it lying flat for a few hours, then hang the coat outdoors again and beat thoroughly until all the powder or bran is removed. Brush thoroughly with a clean brush and the fur will be silky again.

And Now For Your Raincoat

Cleaning a shabby raincoat is another simple process which can be carried out at home.

Dirt and grease collects most around the front edges and the neck of the coat, so it is here that the most attention is needed.

Remove the lining of the coat, wash and press it carefully, as in the case of fur.

Lay the coat itself on a flat table out of doors and with clean soapy water scrub the soiled parts with a stiff nailbrush. Use as little water as possible so as not to swamp the material. Continue this process over the whole surface of the coat, keeping it as dry as possible.

Wash clean of the soap by wiping over the surface with a clean cloth wrung out in warm water. Do not soak the cloth with water.

Oilskin raincoats which have cracked or lost some of their proofing are improved by a treatment with boiled linseed oil.

Apply the linseed oil very thinly to the surface of the coat with a brush. Hang the coat out of doors to dry and repeat the process once or twice more. The drying should take place as quickly as possible, so it is best to choose a dry windy day for the treatment.

Like other commodities, wool supplies were prioritised for military use, and so was also subject to rationing. However, as magazines (and yarn manufacturers) were quick to point out, a woman's sweater made from one of their patterns might only take up two or three coupons, half the amount that would be needed to buy the equivalent item readymade. Woollen garments also had the advantage of being warm (the winters of 1939 and 1941 were particularly cold) and they could be completely unravelled and fashioned into something new. Short-sleeved, multi-coloured jumpers became commonplace as wool from 1930s knitted clothes was repurposed. Sewing a garment from scratch also cost about half as much, and there was an interesting, if limited selection of materials to choose from. In 1941, the Cotton Board commissioned well-known artists including Duncan Grant and Graham Sutherland to design a range of patterns for fabric in a Government-subsidised scheme. Some of the designs were topical such as the famous 'Careless Talk Costs Lives' illustrations by Fougasse. When it came to Christmas, having the skills to sew, make or knit a scarf, hood, belt, placemats or perhaps a sleep mask, was invaluable. Suede and leather were materials that, unusually, were in plentiful supply, though it would have required some confidence to tackle the shoulder bag project published in *Britannia & Eve* in October 1944.

Knitting for the Long Winter Evenings

Warm Woolies... Vest and Pants in a Quick, Easy Pattern, taking only Three Coupons

Britannia & Eve (October 1943)

MATERIALS

6oz. 3-ply Sirdar Super Shetland wool in pale pink and a little contrast colour for edges; Nos. 9 and 11 needles.

MEASUREMENTS

VEST.—Round bust, 33 in.; length at centre front, 22 in.; round hips, 35 in.

PANTIES.—Length, front to crutch, 13 in.; hips, 36 in.

TENSION

7 st. and 9 rows to 1 in.

THE VEST (Back and Front alike)

With No. 11 needles, cast on 120 st. in pink. Work k. 1, p. 1, rib for 10 rows. Change to No. 9 needles and stocking st., and work 2 in. straight. K. 2 tog. at beg. and end of every 4th row until there are 100 st. Work straight until side seams are 8 in. change to No. 11 needles and k. 1, p. 1, rib for 2 in. change to No. 9 needles and stocking st. and m. 1 st. at beg. and end of every 4th row until there are 110 st. Now work the following pattern for 3 ½ in.

1st row.—* K. 2 tog., wl. fwd., k. 1, repeat from * to end, ending k. 1. **2nd row.**—K. **3rd row.**—K. **4th row.**—P.

Repeat these 4 rows.

Change to contrast wool and No. 11 needles and work stocking st. for 8 rows. Cast off.

THE PANTIES (Right leg)

Cast on 118 sts. with No. 11 needles in contrast wool. Work stocking st. for 8 rows. Change to No. 9 needles and pink wool and the lacy patt. For 1 ½ ins. Now work stocking st. and m. 1 st. at beg. and end of every row until there are 130 sts. Now k. 2 tog. on left edge of work only, on every 6th row until there are 115 sts. Now with p. side of work facing, work to within 10 sts. Turn. Work back ; work to within 20 sts. Turn. Work back. Continue to work 10 less sts. on every row until there are 15 left. Now work 2 ins. stocking st. Change to No. 11 needles and work 2 ins. rib. Cast off.

LEFT LEG

Work as right, but dec. for back seam on right edge of work and having k. side of work towards you when shaping top.

TO MAKE UP

Sew up side seams of vest. Hem top. Sew on ribbon. Sew up leg seams and back and front seams. Hem legs. Hem waist and thread elastic.

ABBREVIATIONS

K. = knit; p. = purl; m. = make; s. = slip; st. = stitch or stitches; tog. = together; beg. = beginning; wl. fwd. = wool forward.

No Coupons Needed

Britannia & Eve (November 1942)

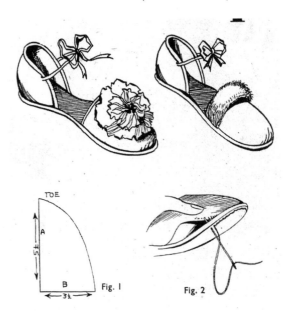

TOE

A

B Fig. I

Fig. 2

Slippers can be made either from felt, which can still be obtained from the stores or an art needle-work shop; from skin, from an old felt hat, or several thicknesses of material with padding, anything, in fact, that your own ingenuity suggests.

Materials required besides are mercerised cotton to match the slipper material, bookbinder's thread for attaching the tops to the soles and some strong ribbon, braid or lengths of felt to bind the edges. For the soles use a strong felt sock or cut them out from several thicknesses of felt stuck together with Seccotine.

To cut out the toe piece proceed as follows:

On paper draw a vertical line 5 ½ ins. long (Fig. 1). Draw another 3 ½ ins. long at right angles from the bottom of the upright. Join the top of the vertical line with the end of the horizontal line. Cut out in paper and lay the pattern on the felt with the vertical line along the fold. Cut for two feet.

For the two backs use the toe pattern again and cut in quadruplicate. Now cut each piece of felt down the centre line "A" shown in the diagram so that the heel piece for each foot is in two sections. Join the sides "B" with a row of small running stitches. Return in the opposite direction with another row of stitches, filling in the spaces left by the first row. Press all seams, using a cloth between the iron and the material.

With a row of short running stitches, beginning about 2 ins. each side of the centre, gather in the toe a little. Similar gathering stitches should be run along the bottom edge of the back, also an inch or more each side of the centre.

Fix the two portions of the upper temporarily to the sole by a thread at the centre back and front of each. Be careful to get the centre backs and fronts in the middle of the sole in each case. Allow a ¼-in. turning for attaching the upper to the sole. Wax the bookbinder's thread before use.

Start at the centre back of the upper to attach the upper to the sole. With a strong needle and the bookbinder's thread, pass the needle through the sole and up through the upper (Fig. 2). Back-stitch right along from heel to toe and then begin at the heel again and continue to the toe on the other side.

Bind the edges of the upper and add a sock for the inside of the slipper to hide the stitches which attach the upper to the sole. The front can be decorated with a flower, as the illustration shows, or with fur. If fur is chosen it should be added before the upper is attached to the sole.

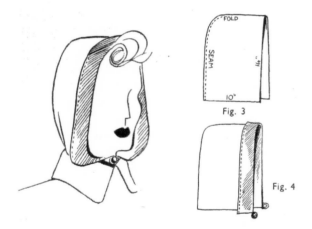

Fig. 3

Fig. 4

Hood Make the hood and mitts to match from any old garment or any length you have of woollen or corduroy velvet material.

Cut a straight length 10 ins. wide by 28 ins. long. Fold in half and seam down one side, rounding one end to shape the crown (Fig. 3). Cut the lining of another colour 3 ½ ins. wider and turn back the edge (Fig. 4). Bind or sew the turned-back edge.

Fasten the hood under the chin with a button and loop. The finished hood is long enough to tuck comfortably into the neck of a coat.

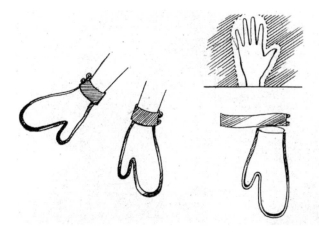

Mitts Use the same materials as for the hood, using the contrasting colour for piping and wristlet bands.

To cut, place the hand on doubled material. Open the fingers slightly and the thumb very wide. Trace round the hand with chalk, leaving ¾ in. for turning. Cut out.

For piping, cut crossway strips of the contrasting material 1 in. wide. Pipe the seams of the mitts with this and machine all round.

To make the wrist bands cut double strips of the contrasting material 2 ins. wide and a little larger than wrist measurement. Join to the top of the mitts, leaving an opening at the outside seam. Fasten with two small buttons and loops.

1. Have you two silk handkerchiefs lying in a drawer? They should be really large, about 28 in. square. Place together, cut to shape, as shown here. Stitch shoulder and side seams, slightly puckering waist. Result, a dressy jumper.

2. Make a leather belt interesting with dropped pockets in matching or contrast material. In the centre of a long, narrow strip, cut out piece, as shown. Fold in half, lengthways, stitch sides and bottom, leaving straps unstitched, turn down flap, and loop on to belt. The two pockets could be cut at the same time.

3. The snood of the moment, made from three passé scarves, joined together and then cut to form almost a square. Place on the head, and fasten two ends beneath the hair, as a nurse ties her white veil. Bring the other two ends up and tie on top

of the head, as shown in the main sketch, arranging the sides in flattering folds. It will keep ears warm this winter.

4. The snood suggestion described above could be glamorously expressed in lace or chiffon, and topped by a little velvet pill-box worn high on the head. This is made out of a round disc about 6 ½ in. in diameter, joined to a straight strip of velvet 9 ½ in. long, 5 ½ in. wide, the whole lined with buckram (and then silk) and neatly stitched together.

5. Berets are everywhere again. Cut a circle in felt or cloth about 9 in. in diameter, cut another circle of the same size, perhaps in fur or fur fabric, for the under part, into which cut a smaller circle, the size of your own head. Stitch together on the outside, and, if you are neat, put in a lining.

6. Match a handled bag to the beret. Cut a piece of fabric 25 in. by 11 ½ in. in the shape shown, and two pieces for the sides, 9 in. long, 2 in. wide. Line, first with buckram, canvas or hessian, then with a piece of silk (cut from anything you have by you). Stitch together, with the side pieces. Large back-stitching is a decorative finish. The flap rolls over and is tied with a remnant of the narrow leather belt which you use for a handle.

7. Cut the entire front from a jumper or cardigan that has had its day, and revive it with a felt or bright woollen waistcoat, made to your size, in the shape diagrammed here.

Make Yourself These String Slippers

Britannia & Eve (January 1944)

MATERIALS REQUIRED

1 crochet hook, 1 pair of cork soles and another pair of fleece-lined ; 2 balls of green glacé string and 1 ball of yellow is sufficient for the tops of 2 pairs ; 1 ball of ordinary white string makes soles for two pairs of shoes. The pattern is for a size 5. Coloured stripes are introduced at regular intervals by changing to alternative coloured string.

STRING SOLE

Begin with white string sole, starting with 12 chain : **1st row.**—1 tr. into fourth ch., 1 tr. into each following ch. to end. Turn with 4 ch. to increase. **2nd row.**—1 tr. into first tr., 1 tr. into each tr. to end, 4 ch. to turn. Repeat previous rows, increasing (with 4 ch.) at each end, following outline of sole until it narrows for instep, then decrease 1 at each end by turning without ch. into second tr. Measure work against the sole until width of instep is reached, continue straight to end of heel.

EXTRA HEEL FLAP

Join white string at instep end of heel, making 1 tr. into each tr. Do plain rows of tr. sufficient to cover heel. Sew firmly down to under-sole at two sides and leave heel end open.

TOP OF SLIPPER

Begin at toe with green string, make 12 ch. **1st row.**—1 d.c. into second ch., continue in d.c. to end, 4ch. to turn. **2nd row.**—1 tr. into first d.c., continue tr. to end, 4 ch. to turn. Continue 5 in. in tr., increasing 1 tr. (with 4 ch.) at each end. Do the last line in d.c. to stiffen. Break off.

FRONT INSERT LOOP

Pick up 10 st. in centre front. Work straight across these in tr. for 12 rows. Cast off.

BACK OF SHOE

60 ch., turn 1 tr. into fourth ch., repeat into each tr. to end, 2 ch. turn. **2nd row.**—1 tr. into first tr., repeat. (Continued on p. 67.)

Leather Permitting

Britannia & Eve (September 1944)

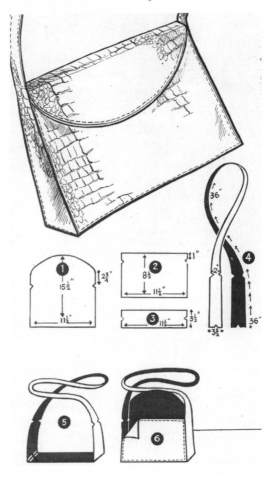

Suède and leather skins are plentiful in the shops, and couponless. This satchel bag is easy to make.

As the skins vary in size, it is advisable to make a paper pattern from the diagram and take it along to the shop, so as to choose your skins accordingly. A half-yard of canvas for stiffening and the same amount of silk is sufficient, if a lining is to be used. This, however, can be dispensed with if the heavier type of skin is used.

Use a glover's needle and strong thread for sewing.

The raw edges of the skin are laid together and sewn with long, even stitches. With the thinner type of skin and most suèdes it is possible to use the machine, which, of course, is stronger and neater, unless you are very accurate with your hand-sewing. When stitching by machine, use a larger stitch than for sewing on fabric.

Following the diagram, draw the outline on stiff paper and cut it out. Now lay the pieces of the pattern on the wrong side of the skin, chalk round them very carefully and cut them out with a very sharp knife or with scissors. Cut the strap double.

If a canvas interlining is being used, cut this exactly the same size as the skin. The silk inner lining should be a half-inch wider all round to allow for turning in.

When using a stiffening, gum the corresponding pieces of canvas to the wrong side of the skins before starting to sew. Use the gum sparingly so that it does not spread over the edges of the skin. Let it dry thoroughly before proceeding.

Before attaching any lining, sew snap fasteners at each corner of the flap front and at corresponding points on the lower front of the bag.

Turn in and press the edges of the silk lining, making each piece fit to the edges of its corresponding piece of skin. Tack at the edges.

Join the two ends of the strap (Figure 4) to the base of the bag (Figure 3), as shown in Figure 5. Make sure that the notches come together. Sew through the three thicknesses of skin, canvas and lining. Next join the front (Figure 2) to the strap and base. Before attaching the back (Figure 1), crease the front flap forward at the notches on either side.

CHAPTER 3
FOOD

It was no secret that food rationing would be an inevitable result of war. With remarkable prescience, the Board of Trade had organised a Food (Defence Plans) Department as early as 1936 and put into place a plan of action for stockpiling non-perishable food and planning out a fair and equal distribution of food in the event of shortages. Although rationing would not be implemented until January 1940, information about how to save food and consume responsibly began to be distributed in the first few weeks of the war. The Ministry of Food, under W. S. Morrison, was established on 8 September 1939 whose first job was to set maximum prices for basic foods in order to prevent profiteering. All British citizens had been required to register on 29 September, with details of all people living in each household, information that would be used for ration cards, which were issued in November 1939. Each household was advised to register with a retailer (usually a local butcher/grocer), which would become the shop where they would exchange their coupons, sometimes for the duration of the war. The system effectively ensured there would be sufficient supplies of rationed foods for everyone. By 8 January 1940, when the first foods – butter, sugar and bacon – were rationed to 4oz per person per week, every effort had been made to ensure the nation's cooks (almost exclusively women) were prepared to deal with the reduced supplies.

In April 1940, Lord Woolton took over as Minister of Food and continued to oversee a campaign of bulletins in the national press, called 'Food Facts' with hints and tips on how to make meals interesting (or merely palatable) and to help rations stretch further. Responsible for ensuring the population's dietary needs were met, Woolton himself sent a message thanking the nation for, 'helping to defeat the enemy's attempt to starve us out', and his high-profile status led to the famous vegetable dish, 'Woolton Pie' being named in his honour.

Throughout 1940 and 1941, as more and more foods became subject to rationing, the quest to find alternatives became a national preoccupation. The British people were being asked to forego what were staple items such as meat and (unthinkably) tea, while the Ministry of Food was concerned with ensuring the nation remained healthy on what food there was. It promoted the virtues of vegetables with the help of characters, 'Potato Pete' and 'Dr Carrot,' and suggested, as alternatives to shortcrust pastry and white bread, potato pastry, and the unpopular 'National loaf', nutritious but coarse and mealy because only 15% of the wheat was discarded. Food economists from the Food Advice Division of the Ministry travelled the country to give demonstrations and share culinary ideas with housewives, and a dedicated BBC radio programme, 'Kitchen Front' was another way to distribute recipes to a wider audience.

Magazines were again an essential tool in offering help and ideas to housewives who were often understandably frustrated; feeding a family was difficult enough without the added challenges of daily queues and having to make something out of very little. In its November 1939 issue, *Britannia & Eve* ran a spread on economical meals such as herrings fried in oatmeal or prunes and barley. It reminded readers to save vegetable water as stock and extolled the benefits of tinned foods. It also regularly published articles concerned with ensuring children received the right nutrition. The rationing system, recognising differing nutritional needs among the population, allocated additional milk and eggs to children and pregnant women, and orange juice, blackcurrant juice, rosehip syrup and cod liver oil to children under five. Among suggestions in the magazine for a juvenile diet, mothers were told not to peel fruit, and recommended to steam vegetables and cook potatoes in their skins. A diet chart from the Ministry of Food was suggested as an accurate way of 'better understanding the principles of feeding.'

The wartime diet was undeniably healthy, but it was often also bland, and magazine recipes offered the opportunity to brighten up mealtimes, even if some required an adventurous attitude. Tripe, stuffed turnips, fish dumplings in curry sauce, creamed dogfish and various types of seaweed were just some of the culinary suggestions made to readers of *Britannia & Eve* during the war. There were also the more typical features on preserving food, and recipes tackling the dreaded dried eggs. Even household pets were not forgotten. Tragically, almost 400,000 pets (mainly cats) were destroyed in the first week of war, but those that remained required food just like their human owners and *Britannia & Eve* offered a no-nonsense list of alternatives for four-legged friends including horseflesh, seaweed and even mice!

"Off the Ration Book"

Britannia & Eve (February 1940)

Of course, most of us are taking the official tip from the Ministry of Food and, as far as we can, still buying the good cuts of meat.

However, an occasional incursion into the unrationed realms of "offal" will help when all the week's coupons have been mortgaged.

The woman who used to shudder at the very mention of tripe now lets her culinary fancy rove around not only tripe, but sheep's head, ox hearts and other portions of animal anatomy.

Most of these things need slow and prolonged cooking. So a good deep ovenglass casserole, capable of taking a pot roast as well as a stew, is a valuable addition to the *batterie de cuisine*. Phoenix produce a round one with a lid that can be reversed and used as an extra casserole; the biggest size (three and a half pints) costs 7s. 6d.

Then there is sugar. If you find that the ration comes hard on you, you can try plenty of dodges for eking it out.

One of the best is to sweeten stewed fruit or puddings with honey (a bit expensive, but good), syrup or jam.

A good trick is to make very thin pancakes and fill them with apples stewed without sugar. A squeeze of lemon juice while stewing improves the flavour.

Fold the pancakes in three and pour hot raspberry jam over. Jam sauce, so sickly when used with a pudding containing sugar, is quite sweet enough as a substitute.

And, of course, you are wise to the device of using sweetened dried fruit like dates and raisins in cakes and puddings.

Although vitaminized margarine is so good and nutritious, we don't say no to ideas for spinning out the butter ration. You can get glass churns which practically double your butter quota by blending milk with it; the result is milky but good.

Here's another simple method. Warm four tablespoonfuls of milk to blood heat. Add it gradually to your flour ounces of butter, beating with a fork, and you will increase your ration to six and a half ounces.

You can also spin out the margarine and make a pretty convincing butter "stand-in" at the same time. To half a pound of margarine take one egg, half pint of milk, one small teaspoonful of salt and one level tablespoonful of cornflour.

Mix the cornflour smoothly with a little of the cold milk, and add to the beaten egg. Put the rest of the milk on to heat with the salt. Add the cornflour and stir till thickened. Leave to cool.

Cream the margarine well, add the cornflour mixture to it and beat all together. This will yield about one pound of butter.

Tripe and Cheese

Many people who say they don't like tripe will enjoy it this way. Buy two pounds of tripe ready prepared by the butcher—it is usually sold partly cooked. Wash it and cut in pieces. Cook slowly in a pan or lidded casserole for about two hours, with water to cover, four or five cloves and seasoning. (Regulo Mark 2.) Now remove from fire or oven and thicken with one ounce of flour and quarter pint of milk. Have ready quarter pound of grated cheese. Scatter this on top and brown in the oven or under the grill. (Regulo Mark 7.)

Sausage Meat Pie

This recipe comes from a woman cookery expert at the Ministry of Food.

You need half pound of sausage meat, quarter pound of mutton pieces (this small quantity will not eat into the ration book), half an onion chopped, two apples sliced, one ounce of breadcrumbs, quarter teaspoonful of mixed herbs, salt and pepper, water; pastry to cover.

Cut up the mutton and mix with the sausage meat, onion and seasonings. Put in a glass pie-dish, adding water to come half-way up the dish. Sprinkle crumbs on top and add a thick layer of apple slices. Cover with pastry, and bake for about three-quarters of an hour.

The pie can be made with beef sausages and beef pieces, either shin or flank. (Regulo Mark 6.)

Hazel Hen in Casserole

These little birds in season now, are nice to serve at a small lunch or dinner party, when you naturally wish to have something off the ration card.

Sprinkle the bird with salt, pepper and a little ground ginger. Put in your covered oven casserole with one ounce of margarine, and cook until tender. Take out the bird and keep it hot. Put in the casserole a cupful of sour cream or top milk, and the juice of half a lemon. Reduce by about a third. Cut the bird into joints and put it back in the casserole. (Regulo Mark 4.) Serve with potato pancakes made as follows.

Grate four raw potatoes. Add salt, plenty of pepper, and two tablespoonfuls of flour. Mix well. Have ready a frying-pan with hot olive oil, drop in spoonfuls of the potato mixture and fry on both sides.

Date Pudding

This is made without sugar. You need six ounces each of plain flour and Atora shredded suet, quarter pound of stoned dates (weighed after stoning), one small egg, quarter pint milk and a pinch of salt.

Sift the flour with the salt and add the other dry ingredients. Mix together. Stir in the beaten egg and milk, but do not beat.

Three-parts fill a greased basin with the mixture, fold a greased paper over the top and steam for four hours. Turn out and serve.

Sugarless Gingerbread

Ingredients are: nine ounces of flour, three ounces of oatmeal, three ounces of margarine, one and a half teaspoonfuls of ground ginger, half a pound of treacle, one teaspoonful of bicarbonate of soda, one gill of milk.

Mix together the flour, oatmeal and ginger. Melt the margarine and treacle and add it. Now dissolve the soda in the milk and pour it in. Mix all together, and bake for about an hour in a moderate oven. (Regulo Mark 3.)

You don't like waste? Neither does any woman who cares about good cookery. Even in peace time I would join battle with the cook who casts into the dustbin that best scrap of fish or that perfectly good mutton bone, instead of pepping it up as a savoury or popping it into the stockpot.

Now that economy is a national duty, we can take a firm line in such matters without being a target for black looks which said, as plainly as plain cooks know how, "Mean old devil …."

And really it's no hardship, but merely a sporting exercise of wits, to have to consider ways and means of utilising every scrap from the larder.

If your little ruse works, and no one remarks rudely "What—mutton again?" you may congratulate yourself on scoring a point.

See that your kitchen cabinet contains a varied array of herbs and flavourings to aid your enterprise. There should be thyme, mace and bayleaves; there should be paprika and celery salt; there should be a bottle of good piquant sauce to add zest to what might otherwise be insipid; and, needless to say, there should always be fresh parsley and shallots at hand.

Poached Egg with Fish

For this, use any white fish left over. Flake it, season and heat in a saucepan with white sauce. Make a slice of toast for each person, and spread with margarine. Put a liberal portion of creamed fish on top and surmount with a poached egg. Add a little tomato puree (canned), scatter with margarine breadcrumbs and brown under the grill.

Fish Rissoles

This uses up cooked fish and potatoes. Skin, bone and flake about half pound of white fish. Put in a basin, and add quarter pound of mashed potatoes, two teaspoonfuls of Lea and Perrin's sauce (grand for adding an exciting flavour) and three ounces of grated cheese, with pepper, salt, made mustard and about one teaspoonful of chopped parsley. Mix together. Beat the egg and add just enough of it to bind the mixture.

Spread on a plate and divide into pieces. Scatter with flour and flour the hands. Shape each piece into a ball. Brush with the rest of the beaten egg, roll in breadcrumbs and fry in deep fat. Drain and serve hot.

Colonel's Curry

This is an easy way of fixing a dish for four people from about half a pound of left-over meat—corn beef if you like, or any other.

Warm a thick saucepan over the fire and put in margarine or other cooking fat. Chop two medium-sized onions and melt slowly, without browning.

Meanwhile, dice the meat and two good-sized apples; chop an outside stalk or two of celery (about a dessert-spoonful). Also take one tablespoonful each of raisins and currants, and wash.

Mix all these together and grate a little lemon peel over. Blend in a cup two dessertspoonfuls of curry powder with enough stock or water to make a thin-cream mixture. (Left-over vegetable soup can be used instead of meat stock.) Add dry ingredients to onions, and stir over a slow fire.

Now mix in curry liquid, adding one tablespoonful of Lea and Perrin's sauce. Put on a slow fire, stirring occasionally. If dry, add a little stock or water. Takes about thirty minutes. Serve with rice.

Water must be boiling furiously before rice is put in. For four people, use a big pan of water and one and a half cupfuls of rice. Salt the water first and add slivers of lemon peel. Add rice slowly and keep stirring meanwhile. When water is just starting to cloud (about twelve minutes) put rice in a colander, strain well, run a dash of cold water through and put colander in the oven. Stir around a bit to heat through.

Serve cut lemon and chutney with the curry.

Potato Cakes

Rub six ounces of dripping into half pound of flour. Work this into one and a quarter pounds of left-over mashed potatoes, which you have heated up, with salt and pepper. Roll out fairly thinly and cut into triangles. Bake in a hot oven or fry in the bacon fat. If baked, spread with margarine. (Regulo Mark 7.)

Salad Suggestion

Left-over rice is a useful addition to salads when fresh green lettuces are not so easy to get. This mixture, in fact, makes use of three "left-overs" for its ingredients. Take three parts boiled rice, two parts diced cooked beetroot and one part diced raw celery, chicory or seakale. Salt lightly and mix with mayonnaise.

Corn Beef Hash

Cold potatoes can be used up in a number of ways but one of the best is corn beef hash which the Americans like so much.

Open a tin of corn beef and chop it fairly small. Mash the cold potato with a little warm milk and mix together with the meat. Season well with salt and pepper. Spread in a well greased frying pan and fry slowly until golden brown. A little finely chopped onion is a savoury addition if you are for it.

"It's in the Cooking"

Britannia & Eve (September 1943)

They used to say a woman could cook if she knew how to boil a potato and make porridge. To these we now add a third test. She must be able to make dried egg taste like eggs and not like wet boot leather. No other wartime food is so dependent on the cooking.

This is the right way with dried eggs:—

(1) Prepare the mixture just before it is required.
(2) Mix the powder (for a rich, creamy scramble) with 1½ tablespoonfuls of water and 1 tablespoonful milk, or household milk, to each level table-spoonful of dried egg powder
(3) Add liquid slowly to powder, as when mixing flour; stir thoroughly with a wooden spoon, leaving no lumps. Whisk well with a fork
(4) Cook the scramble fairly quickly, unlike the slow scrambling which is best for shell eggs.

When the eggs are not to be scrambled and you mix with water only, as per directions on the packet, instruction No. 3 above remains vitally important. So does

No. 1. *Never* leave the mixed egg standing around longer than the couple of hours or so needed for a batter to "rest."

Health experts say that these dried eggs lose none of their food value in the wonderful superhet pulverising process they undergo in Canada and America.

PICNIC EGGS

4 dried eggs (reconstituted); 1 lb. mashed potato; 3 rashers bacon (finely chopped); 2 oz. chopped onion or leek; 1 tablespoonful chopped parsley; ½ teaspoonful mixed herbs; salt and pepper.

Pastry: 12 oz. flour; 4 oz. fat; 2 oz. grated cheese; 2 level teaspoonfuls baking-powder; water to mix; salt.

Reconstitute the eggs, using one tablespoonful more water than usual. Put into small greased moulds or eggcups, and steam until set (about 10 minutes). Cool and unmould. Mix potato, bacon, onion, herbs and seasoning and divide into as many portions as you have "eggs."

Spread on a board, put an "egg" in each portion, and mould the mixture round it.

Make the pastry by rubbing fat into flour, adding cheese, baking-powder and salt, mixing to a stiff dough with a little water. Divide pastry according to the number of eggs and roll out each piece thinly to an oblong shape. Put one of the moulded eggs on each piece, moisten the edges, and fold over, keeping an egg shape. Brush over with milk and bake for 30 minutes in a moderate oven. Serve cold with salad.

PICNIC EGGS

HOT BACON AND EGG SALAD

2 eggs (reconstituted); ½ small cabbage; ½ oz. margarine; ¾ oz. flour; ½ pint vegetable water; 2 teaspoonfuls sugar; 1 teaspoonful made mustard; 1 lb. potatoes (cooked and sliced); 2 or 3 carrots (cooked and sliced); 1 lb. cooked runner beans; 4 rashers bacon (cooked and chopped); 1 onion or clove of garlic (grated); vinegar to taste; pepper and salt.

As in the recipe for Picnic Eggs, reconstitute the eggs with an extra tablespoonful of water, and steam till set in moulds or eggcups. Cool and cut in slices.

Shred the cabbage finely, put in a bowl and pour boiling water over. Leave for a minute or two, then strain.

Make a sauce with the margarine, flour and vegetable water. Add sugar, mustard, vinegar, salt and pepper.

Put a layer of the blanched cabbage at the bottom of a casserole. Add the other vegetables in layers with the rest of the cabbage.

Sprinkle the layers with the bacon and onion and the sliced egg. Finish up with a layer of potatoes on top. Pour the sauce over, and put in the oven to reheat (about 15 minutes). If possible, cover the dish while this is being done. Scatter chopped parsley over before serving.

HOLLANDAISE SAUCE

½ pint white sauce; 4 peppercorns; 3 tablespoonfuls vinegar; 2 eggs (reconstituted); pepper and salt.

Add the peppercorns to the sauce before cooking, and when cooked remove them and stir in the egg mixture slowly. Add the seasonings and reheat, stirring constantly.

This is a useful sauce to serve with vegetables or with fish, and you can use it cold as a salad dressing.

When using dried household milk in cooking it is often easier to add it to the other ingredients dry instead of mixing it with water beforehand.

In the following recipe both the dried egg and the dried milk are used without being "reconstituted" first.

FRUIT CUSTARD

Stewed fresh fruit; 4 tablespoonfuls dried egg; 4 tablespoonfuls household milk (both in powder form); 4 tablespoonfuls sugars; 1 pint water.

Put the fruit in a glass serving dish. Mix the egg and milk powders with the sugar. Slowly add the water, stirring well, and beat until smooth. Cook gently for about 20 minutes, pour over the fruit and leave in a cool place to set. Decorate with grated nutmeg or chopped nuts.

CHOCOLATE SOUFFLÉ

1 oz. fat; 1 oz. flour; 1 gill milk; 4 eggs (reconstituted); 1 dessertspoonful sugar; 1 teaspoonful cocoa.

Not so many people know that you can make a soufflé with dried eggs; you can, and it makes a useful addition to the rather depleted wartime repertoire of sweet dishes.

Melt the fat and stir in the flour carefully. Add the milk, stirring, and cook until the mixture leaves the side of the pan. Add sugar and cocoa. Beat the eggs, add to the mixture, and beat well together. Pour into a greased dish and bake for 15 minutes in a fairly hot oven. Like peace time soufflés, this one won't wait; it must be served at once.

FRUIT FOOL

1 lb. plums or other fruit in season (or ½ lb. dried fruit previously soaked); 2 oz. household milk (in powder form); 1 ½ oz. sugar.

Simmer the fruit gently with very little water and sugar until soft. When cool beat up with a fork, add the milk powder and beat to a creamy consistency. Put into individual glasses and sprinkle with cocoa or chopped nuts to decorate.

FRUIT FOOL

"Vegetable Variety"

Britannia & Eve (January 1943)

The word vegetable has assumed new significance in the kitchen to-day. We used to think it not particularly interesting, just a supplementary background to the important part of the dish. As such, it was often dull and without nutriment because of indifferent cooking. Now that vegetables frequently have to be the main dish, the English have learnt how to cook them so that their essential nutriment is fully conserved and their characteristic flavour properly enjoyed.

Sprouts au Gratin—*1½ lb. Brussels sprouts; little margarine; nutmeg; 4 oz. grated cheese; milk to moisten; salt and pepper.*

Cook sprouts in a little salted water in a lidded pan; drain, and put in a shallow fireproof dish with margarine, pepper and a little grated nutmeg. Sprinkle with grated cheese, moisten with milk and brown quickly under the grill.

Spinach with Rolled Oats—*2 lb. spinach; 2 oz. rolled oats; 2 oz. dripping; 1 teacupful household milk; salt and pepper; grated nutmeg; mashed potatoes.*

Wash and chop spinach roughly. Throw into ¾ pint boiling salted water. Sprinkle in the oats and boil till cooked, when all the moisture should be absorbed. A little more boiling water can be added if necessary.

When oats are done, stir in milk and dripping, and add salt, pepper and a little grated nutmeg.

Keep hot on the side of the stove for about ten minutes before serving in a wall of mashed potatoes.

Cheese and Leek Pie—*6 leeks; 3 oz. grated cheese; ½ breakfastcupful breadcrumbs; 1 breakfastcupful white sauce; 1 tablespoonful margarine; salt and pepper.*

Boil leeks, drain and cut in two-inch lengths. Grease a shallow baking dish, put in two or three tablespoonfuls of the white sauce and then a layer of leeks. Mix the rest of the sauce well with half the cheese, and pour some over the leeks. Repeat the layers with more leeks and cheese sauce. Scatter breadcrumbs over the rest of the cheese on the top, adding dabs of margarine. Brown under the grill.

Cheese Carrots with Sprouts—*1½ lb. carrots; 4 oz. grated cheese; 1 oz. margarine; 1 tablespoonful vinegar; ½ teaspoonful salt; ½ teaspoonful dry mustard; grated nutmeg; pepper and salt.*

Scrape carrots, and cook till soft in a little salted water; drain and mash. Add margarine, vinegar, salt, pepper, nutmeg (one pinch), and cheese. Mix well, stirring over a low heat, until creamy. Pile on a hot serving dish and surround with well-drained Brussels sprouts.

80

Stuffed Onions—*4 onions; ¼ lb. sausage meat; 1 rasher bacon; 1 teaspoonful sugar; dripping; salt and pepper.*

Parboil and drain the onions. Cut a hole through the centre of each and chop the onion thus removed with the sausage meat. Stuff the cavities with the mixture and put in a baking dish with a little dripping. Sprinkle with pepper, salt and sugar. Divide the rasher into four and put a piece on each onion. Bake in a quick oven or under the grill, basting occasionally.

Beetroot Soup—*3 beetroots; 1 head celery; 2 pints milk and water; a little margarine; salt and pepper.*

Boil or bake the beetroots, and when nearly done, peel and chop up. Clean and chop the celery and cook with the beetroot in the milk and water until tender. Pass through a sieve, season to taste, add a little margarine and serve.

Stuffed Turnips—*4 good-sized turnips; 2 rashers of bacon; tomato ketchup; 3 tablespoonfuls breadcrumbs; salt and pepper.*

Wash the turnips and boil them in their skins. When soft, drain and peel them, cut a piece of the top of each and scoop out the middle.

Chop the bacon, which should be cooked, and mix with the cooked, scooped-out turnip, the breadcrumbs, a dash or two of tomato ketchup, and salt and pepper. Stuff the cavities with this, plug it on top of the turnips, and reheat under the grill.

Salsify Sauté—*1 lb. salsify; sprigs of parsley; lemon substitute; salt and pepper; frying fat.*

Scrape salsify and boil until soft. Drain well and cut up into short chunks, dividing the thick parts in two. Fry lightly in hot fat. Sprinkle with salt, pepper and a little lemon substitute. Serve with fried parsley.

Parsnip and Potato Pancake—*1½ lb. potatoes; 1½ lb. sliced parsnips; salt; pepper; frying fat.*

Scrub and boil potatoes and parsnips. Peel, and split the parsnips to remove the hard core. Mash potatoes and parsnips well together, seasoning well. Make the fat hot in a frying pan and put in the mixture in a flat cake. When crisp and brown on one side turn and fry the other.

"Queer Fish"

Britannia & Eve (January 1943)

All sorts of odd fish go into your net bag to-day. Saithe is rather like dark cod with large firm flakes. You may dislike ling because it dries in cooking. Counteract this. Try it filleted in a greased baking tin, covered with bacon rashers, encircled with forcemeat balls. Rock salmon has firm pink and white flesh and a distinctively sweet flavour. Try it grilled or made into pies. Experiment with gurnet, delicious grilled; or plain steamed megrim with parsley sauce.

Ling Soup—*1 lb. ling; ½ lb. potatoes; 1 teacupful household milk and vegetable stock; 1 quart water; 1 small onion or a little chopped leek; 1 oz. cooking fat or margarine; chopped parsley; salt and pepper.*

Clean the fish and cut it up small. Peel and slice the potatoes and onion.

Make the fat hot in a saucepan and put in the vegetables. Saute them for a few minutes, then add the fish and the water, and cook slowly until tender.

Pass the soup through a colander or a coarse sieve, and return it to the pan. Season, add the milk and boil up again. Just before sieving, sprinkle in the chopped parsley.

Rock Salmon with Apple—*1½ lb. rock salmon; ½ lb. cooking apples; 1 lb. parboiled potatoes; browned breadcrumbs; ½ pint white sauce; 1 teaspoonful vinegar; ½ teaspoonful mixed spice; salt and pepper.*

Cut the fish into slices 1½ inch thick. Peel, core and slice the apples, slice the potatoes and put them into a greased fireproof dish, finishing with a layer of apples. Add to the white sauce the vinegar, spice and seasoning. Pour the sauce over the dish, scatter crumbs on top and bake in a moderate oven for twenty minutes.

Baked Skate—*1 lb. skate; 1 breakfastcupful household milk and vegetable stock; 1 tablespoonful margarine or dripping; 1 teacupful finely grated cheese; 1 level tablespoonful flour; salt, pepper and mustard.*

Clean the fish and simmer in salted water until the flesh is nicely set.

In a small saucepan melt the fat, stir in the flour smoothly and cook together until of a honeycomb texture. Gradually add the liquid (milk and stock) and cook, stirring, until the sauce is thick. Season with salt, pepper and dry mustard.

Remove the skin from the fish and bone it. Flake, and put in a greased fireproof dish. Sprinkle with some of the cheese, pour the sauce over and add the rest of the cheese. Bake in a moderate oven for twenty-five to thirty minutes.

Curried Skate—*1 lb. skate; 1 tablespoonful chopped onion or leek; 1 dessertspoonful curry powder; 1 teacupful household milk and vegetable stock; salt; pepper; frying fat.*

Boil the fish and allow to cool. Make fat very hot in a saucepan and add the onion. Fry slowly till light brown, and add the curry powder, dissolved in the household milk. Cook slowly, blending well. Add the fish, cook five minutes more, season and serve. This dish should cook slowly; don't use a fierce fire.

Madras Fish Cakes—*¾ lb. any cooked fish; 6 oz. mashed potato; 2 teaspoonfuls chutney; ½ teaspoonful curry powder; 2 oz. margarine; chopped parsley; salt; pepper; breadcrumbs; frying fat.*

Free fish from skin and bone, and mix with potato, adding chutney, curry powder, margarine and seasoning. Put into a pan and make thoroughly hot, stirring. Take out of pan, allow to cool and form into round, flat cakes. Brush over with a little milk and cover with browned breadcrumbs. Fry until brown. Serve sprinkled with chopped parsley. Fried artichoke "chips" go well on this dish.

Fish Dumplings with Celery Sauce—*½ lb. of any white fish; 1 dried egg; 1 teacupful breadcrumbs; 1 teacupful household milk and vegetable stock; 1 teaspoonful finely chopped onion or leek; 1 teaspoonful chopped parsley; salt and pepper; celery sauce.*

Chop or flake the fish finely. Put the milk in a saucepan, add the breadcrumbs and cook to a paste. Remove from the fire and put in the fish, the whipped egg, the onion and parsley, salt and pepper.

Shape into small even balls about the size of a walnut and cook slowly in boiling salted water for twenty minutes. Drain the little dumplings, turn on to a hot dish lined with well-beaten mashed potato and coat with celery sauce.

Creamed Dogfish—*1 lb. cooked flaked dogfish; 8 oz. breadcrumbs; 2 oz. cooking fat; 4 tablespoonfuls chopped parsley; 1 teaspoonful mixed herbs; salt and pepper; 1 teacupful water; 1 teacupful milk and fish stock; 1 oz. flour.*

Mix together the breadcrumbs, fat, half the parsley and herbs; season with salt and pepper and bind with water. Grease a cake-tin and line it with this stuffing. Bake until nicely browned. Make a sauce with the milk-fish stock mixture and the flour. Stir in the rest of the parsley and the flaked fish.

Remove the ring from the cake-tin and pile the fish mixture into the stuffing case.

Stuffed Fish—This recipe can be used for any whole fish weighing about 2 lb.— haddock, whiting, small cod—or individual steaks of cod, ling, rock salmon or hake.

Cook ½ lb. potatoes and mash them with pepper and salt, and a tablespoonful each of chopped parsley, grated cheese and bacon fat. Bind the mixture with a little of the water in which the potatoes were boiled and, if it can be spared, a little dried egg (reconstituted).

Wash the fish and, if a whole one is used, leave the head on. Split down the front and pack with the stuffing, sewing up the opening with cotton. In the case of the steaks just spread the stuffing on top.

Bake in a quick oven, or fry until brown in a little fat, or cook in fat in a lidded pan on the fire.

"Out-of-a-can Cookery"

Britannia & Eve (January 1942)

Remember the abuse once heaped upon can-opener cooks? They, it was said, cooked not at all; they merely opened a tin, decanted the contents and served.

Now that Lease-Lend has brought American cans of meat and fish and beans into our wartime kitchens, and it is no longer considered unpatriotic to broach a tin from what might be our invasion nest egg, we might do well to lease-borrow a few ways of making over that brisket and rabbit and salmon and pilchard the way they do across the Atlantic when we are tired of eating them as they are.

Variations will readily suggest themselves to cooks with a turn for inventiveness. Meanwhile, here are a few ideas to be going on with. Note that where milk is mentioned, milk powder (prepared to directions) can be used.

BRISKET AND BEETROOT

1 breakfastcupful each of brisket and cooked beetroot (cubed)	1 apple
	Vegetable stock
1½ breakfastcupfuls cooked potato (cubed)	Salt and pepper.
A little chopped onion	

Mix potato and brisket, add onion and season to taste with salt and pepper. Blend thoroughly and moisten with a little vegetable stock. Grease a frying pan and make hot; spread the mixture in this and cook slowly until brown (about half an hour). Fry the beetroot in a little fat in another pan and grate the apple over it in the serving dish. Serve the beetroot with the meat.

FARMHOUSE STEW

½ lb. canned luncheon meat or brisket	1 onion or leek (chopped)
4 oz. haricot beans (soaked overnight)	Vegetable stock
1 tablespoonful pearl barley	1 cube beef extract
1 carrot (sliced)	Salt and pepper
1 turnip or piece of swede (cubed)	Little flour.

Put barley, beans and other vegetables in a pan. Cover with boiling vegetable stock or water, add the cube (crushed) and boil slowly until beans are cooked. Add the meat, cut in cubes. Thicken the liquid with a little blended flour. Season with salt and pepper.

STEAK AND MUSHROOM PIE

1 tin stewed steak
½ dozen mushrooms

6 oz. puff pastry
Salt and pepper.

Open tin and decant the stewed steak into a shallow pie dish. Peel and chop the mushrooms and scatter them over. Season to taste with salt and pepper, and cover with the pastry or potato. Bake in a hot oven about thirty-five minutes.

To make a pie crust without fat, mix 6 oz. wheatmeal flour, a bare teaspoonful of baking powder, a pinch salt, and about ⅕ pint cold milk and water. Roll out and use. Serve hot.

RABBIT AND PRUNE PIE

Use the above recipe for pie, with canned rabbit and six split and stoned cooked prunes instead of steak and mushrooms.

HERRING IN BATTER

4 oz. flour
½ teaspoonful salt
Egg substitute (1 egg)

½ pint milk
1 oz. dripping; pepper
1 small can herrings.

Mix flour and salt, make a well in the centre and add egg. Gradually add half the milk, mixing well. Beat until bubbly. Stir in the rest of milk and leave for half an hour. Make dripping very hot in baking tin. Pour in the batter and add the fish, cut up. Bake in a hot oven until golden brown (about thirty minutes).

BATTER WITHOUT MILK

1 large breakfastcupful of water in which
carrots have been boiled
2 teaspoonfuls custard powder
4 oz. flour

Pinch salt
½ oz. cooking fat
1 teaspoonful baking powder.

This batter, recommended by the Ministry of Food, requires neither milk or eggs. It can be used in the above recipe.

Sieve together the flour, custard powder and salt. Make a well in the centre and stir in one-third of the liquid. Beat well for five to ten minutes, then add rest of liquid. Have fat smoking hot in baking tin. Sprinkle baking powder on top of the batter, to which you have already added the fish, stir very quickly and pour into smoking fat. Let some of the fat run on top of the batter. Bake in a moderately hot oven for twenty to thirty minutes.

SCALLOPED TUNNYFISH

1 can tunnyfish	2 teaspoonfuls parsley
½ lb. creamed potato	Dash Worcester sauce
½ pint white sauce	Salt and pepper.

Flake the tunny and mix with white sauce. Add Worcester sauce, salt and pepper. Put mixture into four or five scallop shells, make a ring of potato round and brown in a hot oven (about ten minutes). Scatter parsley over each before serving.

DEVILLED CRAB

1 shallot (optional)	1 teaspoonful H.P. sauce
2 tablespoonfuls flour	1 teacup milk
Margarine for frying	1 can crab
½ tablespoonful dry mustard	Pepper
Dash of paprika (if available)	Fresh breadcrumbs
A little grated cheese.	

Melt margarine in a pan and cook shallot (chopped) without browning. Add flour, mustard, sauce and pepper, stirring till smoothly blended. Now slowly pour in milk, and cook gently until it thickens, stirring constantly. Stir in the crab meat and put into scallop shells or individual fireproof dishes. Sprinkle breadcrumbs and grated cheese over and, if it can be spared, put a dab of margarine on each. Bake till nicely browned in a moderate oven.

"Out of the Hedgerows"

Britannia & Eve (July 1944)

Starting in early summer, nature opens a useful storehouse in the fields and lanes of things which, if one knows the secret of their preparation, are valuable aids to health, beauty and good eating.

Young nettles, for instance, have a fine food and tonic value. Choose the young heads, wash and cook them as you would spinach, to serve as a second vegetable. Taken for medicinal purposes only, the nettles should be prepared in the form of a syrup.

To make this, boil half a pound of young tops in a pint of water for one hour. Strain off the liquid and add half a pound of sugar, if you can spare it, to each pint of liquid. Boil up again and gently simmer for half an hour. Cool and bottle. A wine-glass of the syrup taken night and morning has a tonic value and is excellent as a blood purifier.

Elder flowers which can be gathered in most parts of the country, make a good softening and whitening hand cream. Melt a quarter of a pound of Vaseline in a saucepan, and add as many elder flowers as can be pressed into it. Simmer the mixture on a very low gas for three-quarters of an hour, then strain immediately and pour into a screw-top jar. Insect bites and heat bumps are pleasantly soothed by this cream.

The fruit of the elder tree can be used to make pies. Treat as for black or red currants. The flavour is richer than that of currants, but very good.

Dried bullace plums make a substitute for sultanas. This wild fruit, which grows very freely in some country districts, should be laid out on trays and put into a cool oven with the door slightly ajar. Leave the fruit for an hour or two each day until all the moisture has evaporated. To save gas, the trays can be placed into the oven after cooking is finished and when the oven is still warm. Repeat the operation every day until the drying process is complete. Another way is to sling the fruit in a piece of muslin or an old lace curtain over the top of the kitchen range. Leave like this for a few days before storing.

Bilberries, which appear in August, make good jam. Prepare them as for other soft fruit, but add a little lemon substitute to give piquancy to the flavour.

Button mushrooms can be picked for winter pickle. Choose the smallest ones, wash and skin them and put them into a glass or stone jar of vinegar to which a few peppercorns have been added. Place in the oven and bring them to the boil. Simmer gently for an hour. Remove and tie down immediately.

Hazel nuts are plentiful in the hedgerows in late summer. Picked ripe they can be stored in airtight tins for eating at Christmas.

Rose hips contain ten to fifteen times as much vitamin C as orange juice. They make a very good sauce to serve with pudding. Prepare the hips as a syrup for this purpose by grating the freshly picked hips and putting them into boiling water. Allow three pints of water to two pounds of hips. Cover and bring them to the boil, then stand aside for ten minutes. Strain through a muslin bag and return the pulp to the saucepan with a further one and a half pints of boiling water. Boil up again for ten minutes and strain. Mix the two extracts and boil again until the liquid measures one and a half pints. Add one and a quarter pounds of sugar, stir until dissolved and boil five minutes more. Fill bottle to within two inches of the top and cork or cover with screw caps. Stand the bottles in water, bring to the boil and sterilize for twenty minutes. Remove and cool.

"Food for the Winter Store"

The Illustrated Sporting and Dramatic News (12 June 1942)

The important job of serving daily food next winter and the next will be lightened if we plan now to preserve all surplus garden produce. With very little trouble all the summer fruits that come our way this year can be safely stored and will be doubly welcome when the growing months are finished. No sugar is necessary with either of the two methods approved by the Ministry of Food. With attention to the few important details, success is assured, so it will be well worth while stocking up when the fruits are in season and while they are fresh.

Apples, apricots, cherries, damsons, gooseberries, loganberries, plums and rhubarb are particularly suitable for bottling by the sterilising process. The fruit should be carefully graded for size and ripeness, put into the preserving bottles which are then filled with cold water. Place them into a deep vessel, making sure that the water just covers the tops of the bottles, and in 1½ hours brought to a heat from between 165 and 175 deg. Fahr., according to the kind of fruit. Make sure that your containers are absolutely clean, and while clip-top or screw-band preserving bottles of the vacuum type are desirable, you can make an air-tight seal with three or four layers of grease-proof paper dipped in a flour-and-water paste.

The wrong way. The pan is too shallow, and because of the alkali content of vegetables they are unsafe to preserve.

After the required heat has been maintained for a period varying between ten minutes and half-an-hour, the sterilisation is complete and the bottles are removed for cooling. When cool, each container can be lifted by the lid to test the seal before being put away. The lid should remain firm after the screw bands or clips are removed, but if it comes off there is a fault in the seal. This may be due to faulty rubber bands. You cannot obtain a good vacuum if there is as much as a pinprick in the bands, so make sure that the tops of the bottle are smooth. If you have been wise, the bands from last year's preserving jars have been washed and kept in an air-tight container while not in use.

Rhubarb should be gathered while young and tender, and can be cut into the size to fit your bottles. You can effect another economy in space by cutting your plums in half and taking out the stones.

Tomatoes. The method with tomatoes is to cover them with brine made from half an ounce of salt to one quart of water. (A very little sugar, about ¼ oz., may be added, but this is not essential.) First having blanched the tomatoes in boiling water for about half a minute, then immerse them in cold water and remove the skins. The tomatoes in their preserving jars are sterilised in the same way after as other fruits, and at the same time, providing the temperature in this case is maintained for thirty minutes.

Campden Solution. There is another way which is even simpler since it requires no heat, although certain fruits are not recommended for this method. Pears or blackberries are best sterilised, also the skins of gooseberries and black-currants are thickened somewhat by the Campden solution method. For this you need fruit-preserving tablets—there are several branded kinds obtainable from chemists—containing 55 per cent. sulphur dioxide. Two of these tablets are dissolved in one pint of cold water and the solution poured over the fruit, which must be well covered and sealed as for sterilisation, and if stored in a cool place will keep indefinitely. There is a condition that the solution is made freshly whenever you are preserving and that the fruit is cooked before being served in order to boil off the preservative. The fruit may lose colour, but this will at least partly return during the cooking process.

"Made to Measure." Rhubarb can be cut into small pieces, or in lengths to fit your bottles.

Clips can be removed when the process is completed. If the vacuum is right the lid will be quite firm.

A deep preserving pan is recommended, and the water must be over the tops of the bottles.

"The Mighty Atom." The Camden solution way with cold water.

Vegetables are not recommended for bottling by these methods, as they require a steam pressure which is not possible with ordinary cooking methods in order to effect efficient sterilisation, since many vegetables may be contaminated with soil organisms including heat-resistant forms of bacteria. We can, however, delight in the fact that our favourite green vegetable—RUNNER BEANS—can be saved quite safely for as long as you like with just an addition of common salt, retaining their colour and, what is more important, the vitamin content.

Gather the beans when young and fresh and tender, and let them dry off for an hour or so. For about 3 lb. of beans 1 lb. of common salt is required. Prepare the beans as though for the table, or you can leave them whole if you prefer, and if they are not too large. See that the jar to be used is perfectly dry and put a good layer of salt at the bottom. It is not necessary to use glass preserving jars for beans; any container will do. If you have a large earthenware crock available, this will be admirable, and if you have paid the initial and after attentions to your crops this year, you will have a heavy yield from early August till October—so your outsize container can be filled easily. Put a layer of beans on the salt at the bottom of the jar, then more salt, filling up with alternate layers of beans and salt, and finishing with salt at the top. Leave several days, as you will find that the beans will sink and there will be room for adding fresh layers. All that will be necessary when you bring them out in the winter months is to soak them for two hours to free them from the salt before cooking in the usual way, and you will have good reason to congratulate yourself on having fallen in line in the modern manner with Mrs. Beeton's sound advice to keep a good stock of preserves.

"Edible and Medicinal Seaweeds"

By W.P. Pycraft, F.Z.S.

The Illustrated London News (27 January 1940)

Most of us, probably, are looking somewhat apprehensively at every source and kind of food which will afford us at least a palatable meal, lest we shall awake one morning and find it "rationed"! But let us not be alarmed. "Rationing" does not mean that we must "tighten our belts," or endeavour to find satisfaction in a diet of sawdust! It means no more than "conservation," so that there shall be enough for us all, even in times of direst stress. And the probabilities of such times over-whelming us are indeed remote!

But "palatable meals" have a wide meaning. And there are many who find such meals in seaweeds! So far as I can gather, however, these rather unusual "vegetables" are rarely, in themselves, regarded as sufficient for either a breakfast or a dinner, but rather as most of us eat pickles, to give savour to a meal.

On the coast of Donegal, where I have spent some of the most wonderful holidays of my life, the seaweed known as "Carragheen," or "Irish moss," is used both for cattle-feeding and for human food. In the latter case, it is first bleached in the sun and then cooked. But it was at one time much used medically as an emulsion, for throat and chest troubles. It is, indeed, still so used, but, my chemist tells me, not so much as formerly, and is collected, for medicinal purposes, chiefly on the northern coast of Brittany. The general appearance of this moss is shown in Fig. 1. The colour, it should be noted, varies from green to purplish-red.

Fig. 1. A seaweed used in the west of Ireland for human food as well as for feeding cattle; the carragheen, or "Irish," moss (*chondrus crispus*), at one time in great demand medicinally and still used for this purpose, large quantities being obtained from the northern coasts of Brittany. Photographs by D.P. Wilson, Marine Biological Laboratory, Plymouth.

The larger species of algae, known as the "brown" seaweeds, afford a useful, though somewhat coarse, form of food, both for human consumption and for domesticated animals. The laver (*Porphyra lasciniata*), eaten both in England and Wales, is by many people regarded as a luxury, though, as with olives, it is not relished at first. After washing, it is boiled for a considerable time, with a slight addition of vinegar. On cooling, it forms a gelatinous mass, and is made up into small cakes, coated in oatmeal, and fried. It is prepared in a very appetising way by the Japanese, who spread it out in the sun until it is dry and brittle. Small pieces are then broken off and toasted over a fire, diffusing a most appetising aroma. It is a far cry from our shores to Japan, hence one feels constrained to ask whether it may not be that the use of laver as food was adopted by us from Japan, as a consequence of the experience of our sailors when visiting Japanese ports in the distant past. For it is to be remembered that though seaweeds are eaten in many countries, the Japanese are by far the greatest consumers of this source of food. They are not content to glean their supplies at low water from the rocks, but will harvest considerable quantities of the broad-leaved laminarian species by tearing it from the bottom by means of long hooks.

The Chinese use a species of *Nostic* as an ingredient of soup, the "bassorin" it contains being much to their liking, and another, *Durvillea utilis*, is also used is soups in Chile. In the Shetland Islands and the Hebrides, dulse (*Fucus saccharinus*) is much liked. It contains as much as 12 per cent. of mannite. The story is told of a Scottish divine who, in explaining the "pulse" diet chosen by Daniel and his three companions, in place of the "king's meat," while they were in training for high office, brought home to his flock the meaning of the word "pulse" by saying: "Brethren, their pulse was our dulse"! In Donegal, and probably other parts of Ireland, dulse is also eaten with relish, but raw. Another seaweed eaten in Ireland is called "sloke," but, so far, I have been unable to find out its scientific name and relationships. My old friend Mr. H. Eliot-Howard tells me it is a "slimy, green weed," and described certain silver saucepans used in the home of his charming wife when she was a girl, living in Donegal, known as "sloke saucepans."

Agar-agar, or Japanese isinglass, is the name of a jelly to be found in all kitchens where good cooking is venerated. It is made from various species of the red seaweeds, which are boiled until a gelatinous residue is produced, and this is used for soups, gravies, jellies, ice-creams and sweets. Even more important is the part it is made to play by the bacteriologist, as it provides him with a transparent, gelatinous medium for the cultivation of disease-causing and other bacteria. But some of these invisible but deadly scourges of mankind will not thrive on this medium, and in such cases beef-tea has to be substituted, in the form of a filtered and transparent jelly.

The coarse, brown seaweeds, known as "tangles," or "oar-weeds" (*Laminaria*), yield that most precious commodity, iodine. The amount obtained is greater in plants growing in deep water, outside the range of the tides, than in those growing near the shore and exposed only during extreme low spring tides. During storms, the deeper-growing plants are torn up by the roots and cast ashore, where they are known, in Scotland, as "drift-weeds." There are three species of these, *Laminaria digitate, L. stenophylla, and L. cloustonii*. All are characterised by their yellow-brown, broad, flattened fronds, often several feet in length.

The more familiar bladder-wrack (*Fucus vesiculosus*) whose fronds are borne up by air-filled chambers, lives where it has to hang for long hours from the rocks when the tide goes down. The channelled-wrack (*Pelvetius*) (Fig. 2), the serrated wrack (*Fucus serralus*), the flat-wrack (*Fucus spiralis*), and the knotted-wrack (*Ascophyllus*) are all closely associated in this habitat. But they each have their "territories," which are determined by the range of the tides. Thus it comes about that, as Dr. Douglas Wilson points out, the higher up the shore a seaweed lives, the shorter the time it is covered by the sea, hence the different species live in different zones. Thus the channelled-wrack is covered only for a short time during high tide. On certain days the sea does not rise high enough to cover it. The flat-wrack, for 80 to 60 per cent. of the time, is left uncovered by the sea. The knotted-wrack covers a wide zone, the upper limit receiving nearly 55 per cent. exposure to sun, wind and rain, but the lower border only 15 per cent. This being so, one would have expected to find evidence of adjustment between the plants of the top and lowermost fringes of the belt. But this does not seem to be the case. The bladder-wrack often grows mixed with the flat-wrack. Sometimes one replaces the other, though why this should be is not known.

Fig. 2. The channelled-wrack (*Pelvetia canaliculata*), which has a great hunger for fresh air, since it will grow only on rock surfaces so high that it is submerged only for a short time during high tide—while on certain days the sea does not rise high enough to cover it.

But all these weeds, when torn from their bases and washed ashore, are carefully carried away—where the supply is plentiful—to be used as manure for the land. This seems to be a characteristic harvest on the west coast of Ireland and the east coast of England; as well as the Orkney, Shetland, and Western Islands of Scotland. Its fertilising effects are said to be especially marked when wheat is grown. But one of these, the bladder-wrack, is put to less ignoble uses. For it is of value medicinally. Its chief constituent is a gelatinous substance, algin, but it also contains mannite, obtained too from the ash-tree, *Fraxinus ornis*. This substance has been used to reduce glandular swellings, but it is now used chiefly as an "anti-fat," forming the basis of most of the much-advertised nostrums of this nature. It has been said to influence the activity of the thyroid gland to a greater extent than any other iodine compound—for the bladder-wrack contains iodine—for the proportion of iodine present. It is also used in the preparing of pills.

Fig. 3. One of the "brown" seaweeds, also used medicinally to reduce glandular swellings and still more as a basis for "anti-fat" preparations: the bladder-wrack (*Fucus vesiculosus*), so called from the large air-filled capsules borne on its fronds to enable the plant to float.

"Wartime Dog Foods"

The Illustrated Sporting and Dramatic News (25 December 1942)

It was computed that some 75,000 dogs and cats were destroyed in London alone during one month of September 1939, largely because their owners feared they would be unable to obtain food for them. Once again dog-owners are wondering about future supplies of food, but it is quite possible that there are in Great Britain inexhaustible sources of dog foods whose merits have only to be discovered and proved.

Jelly made from boiling seaweed.

For example, there seems to be no reliable data on the values of seaweeds and bracken roots. Yet, during the years 1916–17–18, carrageen "moss" proved a standby for many coastal dog-owners, who found that their animals would eat the jelly made by boiling this famous seaweed. (It is very wholesome and is used for making blancmanges, jujubes and various preparations for people suffering from pulmonary complaints. It occurs widely on our shores, and is known locally under the names of Irish or Iceland moss and Dorset weed.) But nothing seems to be known about the best quantities of carrageen for dogs or the best methods of processing this food for inland markets, in order that the widest use might be made of a potential food. Nor is anything known about the inclusion in dogs' rations of bladder-wrack, dulse or layer—three other seaweeds which are, if properly treated, edible by human beings. The most one can safely say is that these seaweeds are rich in mineral salts and would probably have an aperient tendency.

Dogs do not digest bracken easily.

As to bracken roots, it is known that pigs will grub them up and thrive on them, and that badgers also eat them. And during 1916 the Board of Agriculture found that bracken roots could be ground into a kind of flour from which bread for human consumption could be made. So what about a bracken-root dog food? Here care would have to be exercised. Though bracken is rich in protein, its starch and fibre would tend to be constipating, for dogs do not digest fibre very happily. But, properly processed, bracken roots might yield a dog food which would be of real value as one constituent in a dog's diet.

Huskies of the Arctic live on fish.

There is much misunderstanding about what food is liked by dogs and what is good for them. Many people, for instance, think fish a dangerous food for dogs. Yet the toughest dogs in the world, the huskies of the Arctic, live almost entirely on fish! Fish scraps and fish unfit for human consumption may, indeed, be good dog food, and no trouble should arise from its use. If a dog is unaccustomed to fish, make a point of feeding him alone. Then he will be much less liable to bolt his meal or come to grief with the bones than if he is engaged in the common canine practice of an eating race! Again, if you boil fish long enough (say, cods' heads) the bones go soft.

Horseflesh … good for dogs.

The water in which fish has been boiled has some food value and is better than plain water for making gruel. Also, it may render palatable otherwise unattractive yet wholesome foods. This is also specially true of the scrapings and the water from the first washing of pans in which meat has been roasted or fried. Certain scraps— rabbits' heads and poultry heads, for example—which are worth little or nothing as human food, contain a lot for a dog. A sensible dog will grind up and eat all of a rabbit's head except the teeth, and the savoury gravy obtained by boiling poultry heads is so rich that it should only be given in moderation.

Nobody needs to be told that horseflesh and various "offals" good for dogs but not eaten by human beings can be bought from slaughterers and butchers, but it is often forgotten that bullock's blood, which has a high food value, can sometimes be obtained. It does not, however, keep very long.

A little porridge, stretched with skim milk and a handful of wheatings or bran, will make a meal which is much better than nothing for a hungry dog. Potatoes may be employed to make up a dog's feed, but they must be used sparingly. The peel, if clean and boiled, is as good as or better than the potatoes themselves. And here the already-mentioned bullocks' blood or the gravy from a boiled fowl's head or something else of that kind, is specially valuable for making the meal palatable.

They consume mice with relish.

Thought cats will eat rats, dogs as a general rule will not, but they consume mice with relish. (If a shrew is swallowed by mistake it will almost certainly be vomited.) Moles will not be eaten, but hedgehogs (if skinned) and squirrels are both wholesome and much liked by dogs. Toads are poisonous, but frogs and snails are both good food. During the last war some dogs were given quantities of small shellfish, boiled after having been gathered on the shore.

In spring and summer, boiled stinging nettles are of great value as a safeguard against skin troubles, to which dogs on a deficient diet are specially liable, and some dogs enjoy raw apple-peelings, which also have virtue but are now all too rare! If hard times should come, care will have to be exercised lest underfed dogs take to eating filth. A dog which has to live on very "short commons" should be fed only once a day. His hunger is then more likely to be sharp enough to enable him to consume a sufficiency even of unappetising food, whereas if he has two meals he will be more fastidious.

Mealtimes in the pre-war British household would traditionally be a sit-down affair with three meals a day around a table. But with men away fighting and many women involved in war work, volunteering or in the armed services, wartime schedules meant that meals were often eaten on the go. One government scheme to provide for this need were British Restaurants, closer to canteens in style and function, which were set up in prefabs and requisitioned public buildings at locations around the country. Generally staffed by volunteers of the W.V.S., they offered good, nutritious meals at a fixed price. "We can't all lunch out every day, and unless there's a British Restaurant handy, it comes a bit expensive," wrote Harriet Muir in July 1942, before going on to suggest fish and gooseberry salad or American-style open sandwiches as a quick lunch option.

Alternatively, women office workers might need to take a packed lunch to eat at their desk, especially as shortened office hours meant going out for a break was often impossible; *Britannia & Eve* duly offered recipe ideas to keep the hunger pangs at bay for this new section of the workforce, and advised on how to wrap and transport food.

"Lunch in the Office"

Britannia & Eve (January 1941)

Packing up snack meals has become part of the day's work, even in a month not usually associated with picnics. Many offices with early closing hours have adopted the eat-at-your-desk plan; and in such cases it is usually better to take something from home than to rely on the ideas of the office boy, who is apt to bring in a doorstep sandwich from the nearest pub.

If you are living in the country you will find, too, that snack lunches must be packed for the children to take to some distant school.

Then, of course, there are the A.R.P. workers to be thought of.

Meals from home are grand when you get there, but often a nuisance to transport unless proper provision is made for their journey. In the absence of greaseproof paper packets that can be slipped into a man's overcoat pocket—a risky way of taking food about, anyway—you have to think of something better.

For a man I would suggest one of those natty brown leather cases sold for army officers, containing a couple of sandwich tins. Cases which include a vacuum flask can be had, too.

Myself, I would prefer a good big leather shopping-bag affair, roomy enough to take a gas mask, a sandwich tin, and maybe a vacuum flask.

The children, of course, have their satchels or attaché cases.

Wrap sandwiches in a damp cheesecloth before putting in the tin. Pastry should be wrapped in a dry cloth.

Some people have a prejudice against sandwiches, mainly because nothing is more dreary than a badly made one. Also because most providers of sandwich meals omit the fresh element so essential to healthy diet.

Tomatoes or fruit should be included separately in the luncheon packet. Or use grated raw carrot, or shredded raw cabbage in the sandwiches themselves. Put in some fried fruit occasionally—figs, dates or raisins.

The recipes given here include soups for the vacuum flask, some unusual sandwiches and variations of the Cornish pasty, one of the most convenient, easily carried and sustaining snack meals you can have.

Potato and Vegetable Soup

Required: ½ oz. each of dried haricot beans, split peas and lentils; 4 good-sized potatoes; 3 carrots; ½ turnip; 3 or 4 leeks; 4 pints water; salt and pepper.

Soak the dried vegetables overnight. Peel the potatoes, turnips and carrots and cut into dice; cut up the leeks. Put all in a saucepan with the water, season, and simmer for about 2 hours, replenishing the water as it reduces. Strain, but do not rub through the sieve.

Sandwich Suggestions

Mock Crab. Made by beating together 4 tablespoonfuls grated cheese, 1 tablespoonful creamed margarine, 1 teaspoonful anchovy paste and pepper.

Pork. Thin slices of cold pork with apple sauce mixed with a dash of chutney.

Herring Roes. Roes, canned or fresh cooked, mashed with mustard, salt, pepper, and a few drops of salad oil and vinegar. Brown bread is best for these.

Liver. Cooked liver minced with a little onion or leek. Scatter with grated raw carrot after spreading.

Cream Cheese. Cream cheese with a dash of tomato sauce, mixed with chopped celery.

Cole Slaw. Shredded heart of raw cabbage marinaded in oil and vinegar for a few hours. Scatter with chopped parsley or chervil after spreading.

Three Sweet Sandwiches. Banana mashed with chutney; chopped nuts and prunes; figs, minced and mixed with chopped nuts or chopped raisins.

Cornish Pasties

Required: ½ lb. flour; ½ lb. steak; ¼ lb. margarine, beef dripping or lard; 2 potatoes; 1 onion; salt and pepper; water.

This is the classic recipe for Cornish pasties. It is enough for two large ones, but for snack lunches it is more convenient to make four pasties with these ingredients.

Rub fat into flour. Put in the salt and a little water, and mix to a stiff dough. For small pasties, divide into four parts, rolling each piece into a thin round. Chop the potatoes, onion and meat, mix them with salt and pepper, and put a layer on one half of each round of pastry. Fold over, and pinch the edges together. Bake in a moderate oven for forty-five minutes.

Other Pastry Fillings

Salmon. 1 small tin salmon; 2 tablespoonfuls cooked potato; 1 tablespoonful minced onion (or leek) and parsley; 1 heaped teaspoonful shredded suet; a few drops anchovy essence; pepper; milk.

Mix all dry ingredients together, add anchovy, moisten with a little milk, fill pastry and bake.

Cold Beef. 3 tablespoonfuls diced or minced beef (roast, stewed or grilled); 2 tablespoonfuls cold potato, 1 dessertspoonful sweet chutney; 1 teaspoonful shredded suet; grated horseradish; gravy or meat extract; salt and pepper. Mix all dry ingredients together and moisten with a little gravy or meat extract.

Cold Mutton.—Diced or minced mutton and cold potato mixed with either cold onion sauce, or red currant jelly and gravy, or cold mint sauce.

Curry.—1 large apple; 1 small chopped onion; fat; a few currants and sultanas; a little flour; 1 teaspoon (level) curry powder; 1 teaspoon brown sugar; ½ teacup milk or stock.

Peel, core and slice the apply and fry in a little fat with the currants and sultanas until golden brown. Add a sprinkling of flour and stir well. Meanwhile, mix curry powder and sugar with the milk or stock. Add this to the mixture. Stir all together over the fire until it is of a fairly firm consistency.

CHAPTER 4
KEEPING UP APPEARANCES

Beauty on duty was a mantra often repeated throughout the war and it was a potent patriotic gesture to put one's best face forward, however trying the circumstances. Clothes might be in short supply but a made-up face with bright red lipstick was a defiant symbol of women's determination not to forsake their femininity. Propaganda posters urging women to join the factories or one of the armed services invariably featured a picture of groomed glamour, further propagating the notion that war work need not interfere with a feminine appearance, and that looking good could contribute in its own subliminal, psychological way to victory. *Britannia & Eve* published its own confirmation of this with an article which, without irony, matched different make-up shades to the specific uniform women were in. Helena Rubinstein's 'Rose Pink' shade was considered flattering for a member of the F.A.N.Y.S. whereas Yardley's 'Vivid' was recommended for the A.T.S. Housewives were encouraged to keep up appearances too; essential in maintaining a positive frame of mind. It was also considered important, and morale-boosting, for women to make every effort to be fragrant and attractive for men, especially those who were returning home on leave.

Advertisements for beauty products continued to proliferate in women's magazines even if supplies could not match pre-war levels (many cosmetic brands devoted a percentage of their manufacturing to munitions or similar through the war). High-end brands such as Elizabeth Arden took up full pages in *Britannia & Eve*, while smaller adverts promoted Peggy Sage, Revlon and Tangee lipstick. At the same time, mindful of the difficulties in procuring beauty products, magazines were on hand with substitutes to try from castor oil for silky and abundant eyelashes to warm olive oil as a face cleanser. And in a bossy tone, the magazine insisted that shortages were no excuse for slovenliness with long check lists asking if uniforms were always brushed at the end of a shift, or if toothpaste and deodorant were used regularly. The latter issues came more cruelly into focus when the Americans entered the war and there were inevitable comparisons between English girls, who had very little (and often very little access to regular baths), and American girls, who had a bountiful array of products at their disposal.

Beauty on Duty

Britannia & Eve (November 1939)

Most women in uniform make two mistakes about their faces. Either they do nothing about them, or they do too much.

There are exceptions, of course. And the exception is a refreshing sight for sore eyes.

She has not cut her hair too short, neither does she wear it dangling on her shoulders. Her skin looks matt, but not powdered. Her lipstick may be bright as a flag, but it does not clash with the scarlet piping of her A.F.S. uniform.

In a peaked service cap, the mouth is terribly important. For the cap does two things to the face. It shadows the eyes, and focuses attention on the lips. The mouth, then, should always be made up with special care.

Unless there is time to make up your mouth with due care, forget your lipstick: better no colour than a smeary too much of it. The same applies to rouge. Use it with discretion, remembering that cream rouge stands up to duty better than dry rouge.

Eye make-up is out of place unless very adroitly done. This does not mean that the eyes should be neglected. They should be bathed daily with eye lotion (drivers, especially those who do a lot of blackout work, will find immense relief by wearing ready prepared eye-pads over the eyes, in their resting moments in the drivers' room). The lashes and brows can be groomed with Vaseline or special cream; the brows should be kept neat but not severely plucked.

Heavy powder foundations should be avoided like the plague, but some kind of base for powder is necessary, both for protection and to avoid the risk of over-powdering or of having to re-powder constantly.

Elizabeth Arden has designed a compact pigskin service kit in a size that conveniently fits into uniform pockets. Contents are fluffy cleansing cream, Velva cream, ultra amoretta foundation cream, lipstick, powder box, comb and mirror.

In emergency, a refresher pad can be used as a powder base. Cleanse with one pad, dry with tissues then pass a fresh pad over the skin and let the moisture dry on before powdering. A tin of these ready-prepared pads, some tissues and a small quantity of your powder foundation should find a permanent place among your service kit. With this ammunition handy a quick clean-up and re-make-up are possible wherever you are.

FOUNDATION	ROUGE	LIPSTICK	POWDER	UNIFORM
Natural Cream *Yardley's*	Vivid	Vivid	Deep Peach	**A.T.S.** (Khaki, brown shoes, brass buttons)
Town and Country *Helena Rubinstein*	Rose Pink	Rose Pink	Peaches and Cream	**F.A.N.Y.S.** (Khaki, brown belt, bronze buttons) **W.A.A.F.S.** (Horizon blue, black, grey stockings, brass buttons)
Honey Bloom *Jane Seymour*	Honey Bloom	Honey Bloom	Honey Bloom	**W.R.E.N.S.** (Navy, black and brass buttons)
"All Day" (Rachel) *Elizabeth Arden*	Stop Red	Stop Red	Matt Fonce first, then special Matt Fonce	**A.F.S.** (Navy, black, sliver buttons, red piping)
Rachel Day Lotion *Cyclax*	English Rose	English Rose	Rose Rachel	**V.A.D.,** Military hospitals; **C.N.R.,** Civilian hospitals. (Butcher blue dress, white apron, handkerchief cap with red cross, navy top coat, black buttons) **St. John Ambulance** (Black suit, silver badges)
Burnt Sugar (Special Rachel) *Elizabeth Arden*	Burnt Sugar	Burnt Sugar	Dark Rachel over special Matt Fonce	**W.V.S.** (Dark green suit, overcoat and hat, trimmed coral ribbon, coral skirt)
Cream of Roses (Brunella) *Innoxa*	Clair	Clair	Olivette	**A.R.P. Warden** (Cinnamon brown dungarees, tin hat)

Raymond's new astrakhan hair-cut is practical, feminine, easy to keep. The hair is cut shortish over the head, permed, curled, carelessly combed through

Makeshift Make-up

By Chrysis

Britannia & Eve (July 1941)

Here are some simple substitutes for beauty aids in case you run short and have to wait for your favourite preparation.

Lash Grower

Castor oil slipped along the roots of the lashes grows them and bestows a becoming gleam: to feed the lids and prevent them from shrivelling, precede the castor oil by a streak of olive oil. To grow lashes longer still, mix castor oil and almond oil. Use the minimum.

Bracing Lotion

One teaspoonful of spirits of camphor in a quart of water gives a face-rinse that whitens, tightens and enlivens the skin, but it is drying and cannot be used more than once a week, say before special outings, or it will parch the skin. In any event, counteract the over-stimulating effects of this tightening by soaking the face in olive oil later at night.

Face Cleaner

Olive oil, a dessertspoonful, warmed till it reaches the fluidity of milk, removes make-up as effectively as any cream. Pass it over the face on finger-tips and wipe clear with cotton wool wrung out in water. Distilled extract of witch-hazel is the toning lotion *par excellence* after this. The same amount of olive oil should be used as a skin-food three times a week after a soap and water wash. After massaging in the warm oil, hold a towel-covered hot water bottle to the cheeks and forehead, then bury the face in a towel that has been wrung out in cold water. The heat ensures assimilation and takes away stickiness, the coolness closes the pores.

Skin food for alternative nights: zinc ointment. A smear only, patted well in.

To Hide Spots

Tip a spirits of camphor bottle to the cork, and dab the cork on the blemish. The liquid will dry in a white film; it will also draw out inflammation in the shortest possible time and cure any eruption, including a cold on the lip.

To Bleach

Wipe sun marks with cucumber rind. If possible, bind it on. The rind is especially soothing to hands and arms. If face and neck have been badly burned, lie down with thin slices of cucumber pulp massed over it.

Cucumber juice is as effective as the pulp and can be bottled. For this, place the thinnest slices on a slanting board, pound them and let the juice drip into a bowl. Dab it on the face and keep dabbing till dry. To allow any juice or liquid to dry by evaporation coarsens the skin.

Whip the juice into zinc ointment, till the latter has reached the consistency of milk, and use it as a bleach feed. No cream will bring tan to a mellower tone, or so completely refine the skin.

Lettuce Mask

After a good soap and water cleanse, cover the face and neck with slightly bruised lettuce leaves, paste these to the skin with the white of an egg, whipped. Lie down for twenty minutes. Then remove the mask by submerging the face in bath-towelling that has been wrung out in hot water. Be sure all albumen is taken off, puff out the cheeks, twitch the nose, exercise the face muscles. Flick in a touch of the cucumber and zinc skin food, wipe, and note the all-round brightening.

Yeast Mask

Buy three pennyworth of yeast and drip in enough milk to make a thick paste. Layer it evenly over your face after it has been cleansed and thinly coated with skin food. Start paste-layering from the base of the neck, contouring carefully to the temples, and fill in from the nose out. On most skins this mask will peel when the good work is complete, but it can be assisted to do so after thirty minutes by steaming towelling. Wipe thoroughly.

Mould lusciously with cucumber and zinc skin food and wipe this away after ten minutes with witch-hazel. The face is now ready for make-up; it will be set firmer, fairer, and younger.

On Duty and Off

By Jane Gordon

Britannia & Eve (October 1943)

It is a bit hard on the English girls, after four years of war, to find themselves compared with American girls, and the "pin-up" variety at that. We have been told that English girls fail to make the most of themselves, but in spite of this we have been assured that the Americans find English girls charming. You can tell with half an eye that the sentiment is reciprocated. I spent some time in the States back in 1939. I studied beauty treatments given in New York, Boston Washington, Chicago and Hollywood. I watched the movie stars working on the sets, lunching in the studio canteens, and I met them at various parties. I watched college girls and jitterbugs, glamour girls, stenographers and shop girls. I also had the chance of seeing my own friends and relations once more. So when it comes to a question of comparing English and American girls, I feel I know what I am talking about.

No other country understands mass production as it is understood in America, and this includes everything used by women, from lingerie to fur coats, hair pins to nail varnish, and ice boxes to table silver. True, the American woman is more pampered than any other woman in the world, but she is also better groomed. She takes endless trouble about the smallest detail. Here is the type of quiz that is frequently checked over in the States by American Girls.

1. Are your comb and brush always clean, your powder-puff spotless?

2. Do you brush your teeth twice a day and use a mouth wash? (A coffee-spoonful of salt in half a tumbler of clear warm water makes an excellent mouth wash.)

3. Do you give your nails a little daily attention, keep the tips clean and white, smooth the edges with emery board, and push back cuticles with a smear of oil or Vaseline?

4. Do you shampoo your hair before it looks limp and oily?

5. Do you brush your hair thoroughly every day?

6. Do you go over your clothes once a week and see that they are mended and brushed, cleaned, pressed and polished?

7. Are your handbags immaculate inside as well as out, or are they dusty with powder, stained with lipstick and spattered with little bits of tobacco?

8. Is your powder compact and lipstick case spick and span?

9. Do you ever start out with a crumpled handkerchief or slightly grubby gloves?

10. Do you go round with lipstick on your teeth or powder on your shoulders?

11. Do you use pins instead of sewing on hooks and buttons?

12. Do you ever check up on your posture? The way to do this is to stand against a wall, feet apart, knees slightly bent, arms at shoulder level, bent at the elbow, and backs of the hands flat on the wall. Push the small of the back to the wall, at the same time drawing in the abdomen. Now slide your arms up as far as you can without hollowing your back. Relax and repeat five times. This is a good chest raiser, as well as fine for posture.

Even if you are young and as pretty as a picture the chances are that you are no "pin-up" girl. It is unlikely that your picture appears in magazines and tabloids, and though every young woman may have a little sneaking feeling of jealousy for this type of glamour, she'd probably rather have her photograph or snapshot cherished exclusively by one particular man. If you are going to have your photograph specially taken for this purpose here are some hints that you may find useful.

When making-up for the photograph be particularly careful not to use cheek rouge, because red comes out black in a photograph and the rouge would give you dark spots on the cheeks. Too light a shade of powder gives bad results, and the powder must, of course, be very fine. Use your lipstick extra lightly for the photograph, and be sure that the outline of your lips is not smudged. Before you keep your appointment with the photographer, check up on your eyebrows and pluck out any hairs that grow out of line. If you still have a little mascara, keep it for this one occasion. Do not have your hair set the day your photograph is to be taken, but at least three or four days previously. Above all, when you find yourself in front of the camera don't try and assume the expression that you consider most becoming or the effect will look horribly posed. It is hard to relax and look natural in front of the camera, but talk in a friendly way to the photographer and you will find you lose a lot of self-consciousness. If you can kid yourself into thinking that he is just taking snapshots of you the result will probably be perfect.

You may not agree with me about this, but I think that Englishwomen wear their uniform better than the American women. The actual uniform may not be as well cut; the skirts are inclined to be too short and too tight. Our stockings are not such good quality as the American stockings. But an Englishwoman wears her uniform with perfect assurance and with no trace of self-consciousness.

Here is a uniform quiz. Examine your conscience on these questions. Allow yourself a maximum of ten for each answer and see how much you can add up to.

1. Do you keep your hair clear of your uniform collar?

2. Have you a coat-hanger for your uniform jacket, coat, dress or uniform?

3. Do you button your jacket when you hang it up and make sure that the hanger is properly fitted into the shoulders?

4. Do you always brush your uniform when you take it off?

5. Do you look for spots and stains at least once a week and deal with them appropriately?

6. Special for girls in camps and war nursery workers. Do you keep a small tooth comb and use it at least once and preferably twice a week?

7. Is your hair always as glossy and sleek as it can be?

8. If you wear an indoor cap, is it invariably spick and span? Nothing looks worse than a grubby, crumpled white cap.

9. Even if your stockings are not fully fashioned, are they invariably fresh, well aired, and worn without wrinkles?

10. Do you use a deodorant can every day (and even if you cannot get your favourite brand such as Arrid, Mum, Odorono, remember that a few drops of Dettol in the rinsing water will ensure under-arm freshness and happy feet)?

Lovely Hands

By Chrysis

Britannia & Eve (February 1940)

Every woman can have fragile-looking hands—however hard she works and whatever their natural shape—provided she knows what tricks to use.

Sympathetic nail-tone cannot help but lengthen the shape, a dissenting note on the finger-tips must inevitably cut it. Brown hands, for instance, should not wear a bluey-red cyclamen nail-polish. An orange or ochre-red will suit them better, one that is dusky and not too vivid. White hands can take any nail-tone. Deep and glowing varnishes are flattering, but choose them with discretion and match them meticulously, not only to the shade of your clothes, but to the skin-tone of your hand.

Close-fitting, even cuticles are the hall-mark of a beautiful hand. They sensitise the appearance of any finger. Only ignorant manicurists ever snip a cuticle nowadays, as they can be shrunk back and kept permanently smooth by a mere drop of cuticle oil, slipped over the base of the nail with a paint-brush. If you do this each time after you wash, you will have a perfect nail-frame. It takes less than half a minute, but if you cannot remember to oil during the day, at least oil before you go to bed. Peggy Sage Cuticle Oil is the one I recommend. This product of a New York specialist cleverly combines astringent and lubricating properties. The skin remains taut, but never cracks.

A clean nail is another essential. You may think this hardly needs mentioning, but far too many women are careless over cleaning under the projecting shards of their nails. An ordinary nail-brush chips varnish, but secretions cannot be allowed to collect under the impression that a brilliant nail over-hang cloaks a multitude of sins. A fastidiously clean under-nail is a telling touch. Thoroughly brush under it with Nail Dress by means of a stiff paint-brush. Nail Dress is a cream which is also a soap, it bleaches the nail-point and serves to accentuate it; it will also remove stains from the upper surface and prolong the colour-life of the varnish. From Peggy Sage again.

Here are all-important secrets on how to manage the nails in order to obtain that filbert shape which transforms a square and spatulate hand into one that appears to be long and tapering.

Never file the nails down the sides to the cuticle under the notion that it emphasises a thin or fine point. It merely broadens the look of the nail. A nail will seem narrow according to the length it can show above and away from the sides, even if the tip is a semi-circle and not a point. The moon at the base of the nail should be carefully arched to follow the same line as the tip. The illusion of slenderness this creates is vital.

A white hair-line, cause by wiping the varnish off the extreme edge, casts a high-light halo which elongates. These, then, are the three chief factors. Another point of significance is the health and resilience of the nail, which is immeasurably increased by systematic buffing before varnish is applied. This brings up the circulation to feed the nail. To and fro rubbing is no use at all. Buff one way only, up.

Hands need not be snow-white to look delicate, but they must be one-colour and smooth. This is difficult to achieve in February, when cold weather often turns them red, immersion in hot water makes them look boiled, and even the minimum of manual labour swells the knuckles and wrists inordinately. A good cream massage helps this condition. There is a special midday cream for the before-lunch wash, which will draw out all tiredness and magically dispel numbness, if passed firmly over the knuckles, down the hands and over the wrist. It re-forms the hand, there is no other word for it.

Two lightning whitening remedies are (*a*) cream which is instantly absorbed and leaves a fine surface; (*b*) a hand-mask which takes fifteen minutes to transform a hand that has become a ham through rough usage into something approaching a lily. Neither of these two remedies will be necessary if you will only make a habit of using the Hand Massage cream daily and supplement it with a strongly smoothening cream twice a week at night. The latter—and all the rest—comes from Peggy Sage; it is perfumed, does not grease-mark the sheets, and there is this strange fact about it—the wearer's hands are never ungraceful, maybe because its particular perfume lends self-confidence.

New Varnishes

Mantilla	An acute blue-red. Highly romantic. For pale hands that have a dark undertone.
Fez	A clear, sharp red. Dazzling with black, white, browns. For blondes.
Nosegay	Pastel, yet definite and attractive. For the grey-haired and conservative and those who like the exquisite.
Regency	A flesh tone, which gives discreet groom. Ideal for uniforms.

'I sit eight hours a day and feel my hips spreading.' This was just one of the readers' problems shared with 'Chrysis' the beauty editor of *Britannia & Eve*. Fitting exercise into a busy routine was difficult but like every other aspect of wartime life, was advised as essential to keeping healthy, fit and able to contribute to the war effort. While manual workers required relaxing exercises, those who carried out sedentary jobs were given more rigorous workouts. The magazine also recognised the problems of finding space and perhaps privacy to carry out exercise when living in shared and often cramped accommodation. Other articles reminded readers of simple healthy habits that could be incorporated into the daily routine. Suggestions such as drinking water regularly or walking briskly after work could be tips taken from the pages of a 21st-century magazine.

Manual Workers/Sedentary Workers

Britannia & Eve (November 1942)

Manual Workers

If your daily war work is of the sterner kind you need relaxing exercises to keep the body supple and the muscles flexible.

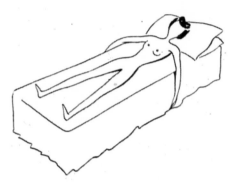

Lie flat and close your eyes, breathing deeply and evenly. Concentrate one by one on all the muscles of the body, relaxing each as you think of it. Let the neck muscles go slack and loose. Follow with one hand and arm. Now the other hand and arm, and so on down to the toes. This needs practice. Hold the relaxed position for at least ten minutes. Be a piece of putty.

Do this one before you get into bed. It starts the process of relaxation: Stand upright, feet apart. Raise arms over head, then relax everything and flop loosely forward until the finger-tips reach the floor. Do the movement in rag doll fashion. Raise up and repeat six times. Breathe in as you raise the arms, out as you flop forwards.

This exercise is good for balance generally. Stand upright, stomach in, shoulders down, arms loose at the sides. Swing the arms backwards and forwards with relaxed shoulder muscles, breathing in and out deeply as you work. After a few swings, continue the movement through and over to describe a full circle. Hold a weight in each hand as you do it.

This exercise is good for a thickening chin. Stand with chin drawn in. Open the mouth wide and let the head fall backwards. Now close the mouth and, with the chin held in tightly, slowly draw the head upwards to the natural position. Repeat twelve times.

To prevent thickening of the waist and spreading seat: Stand upright with feet apart and hands hanging loose. Bend forward with the body relaxed and carry the trunk round to the left, bending backwards as you go and continuing until you have described a full circle. Breathe in and out slowly and deeply as you move. Keep relaxed with the stomach held in.

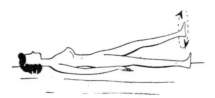

People who stand at their work need foot exercises to strengthen the arches and prevent congestion around the ankles. Hold the leg off the ground. Rotate the foot clockwise six times, then anti-clockwise six times more. Repeat with the other foot. In the bedroom when your feet are bare, try picking up a pencil with the toes.

Sedentary Workers

If you sit at your war work your body and circulation need stimulation. These exercises done regularly each day will achieve this.

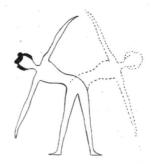

Stand upright with the feet apart, hands outstretched at the sides. Bend slowly over to the left and keeping chin and stomach drawn in, touch the floor with the fingertip if possible. Raise up again and repeat on the right side. Breathe out as you go down, in as you come up.

Lie flat on the floor with the feet together. Keep the arms on the floor and raise one leg upwards as high as possible. Slowly lower again and repeat with the other leg. After three times with each do the exercise with both legs together. Breathe in deeply with the upward movement and outwards as the legs are lowered.

Stand erect with finger tips on the shoulders. In this position raise the elbows as high as possible until they are level with the top of your head. Now lower them to the first position. Breathe in with the upward movement and out with the lowering one. This is one of the best exercises known for the shoulder and breast line.

Stand upright with the feet apart, arms outstretched to the sides. Bend forward, bringing the right hand down to touch the left toe. Raise up again and bring the left arm to touch the right toe. Repeat this exercise rapidly a number of times, taking care to bring the body quite upright after each bending movement.

Lie flat with the toes hooked under a chair or a piece of heavy furniture. Put the hands behind the head and draw up to a sitting posture by exerting pressure on the toes. Do the movement slowly and return slowly to the flat position. Count three as you breathe in and three as you breathe out, keeping breathing deep and regular.

Lie face downwards on the floor with your hands flat on the floor in front of you. With the hands, push the trunk strongly upwards and backwards as high as possible, without raising the lower part of the body. Resume the flat position slowly and repeat six times. Breathe in as you raise the trunk, out as you lower it again.

Exercising in Secret

Britannia & Eve (October 1943)

Privacy is a thing of pre-war vintage. The number of women who write to say that they cannot exercise because they are in the Army, or sharing digs or sharing a room with some blitzed relative, make it necessary to unearth those exercises that can be done secretly. Of course there are few people who cannot get a moment or two in the bathroom, so don't use these exercises if you can possibly work other more energetic ones, but if you are stumped and must improve that figure, here are the places that can be trusted surreptitiously.

Eyes You are reading, or working at something close to your eyes; stop for a moment and look out the window to the most distant object in your view. Look at it concentratedly for a minute and then return to the close-up. Repeat this long and short distance several times each day, blinking in between. Keeping the head still, roll the eyes, gaze from side to side, look up, look down, look N.E., S.W., N.W., S.E.

Chin Instead of the old elbows on table, chin on hands posture, make those hands into a ridge of clasped knuckles and rest the double chin on them; then with chin held up, and shoulders straight, chest forward, rock your head slowly from side to side. It may look like some new annoying mannerism, but no one will guess (unless they have read this too) that you are letting knuckles massage away double chin, and exercising the neck as well.

Bust Fold your arms behind your back, and then slightly raise first one shoulder and then the other, keeping your chin well back all the time.

Or, lying in bed arms clasped over your head on the pillow, push first one elbow and then the other away from your head; if you do it correctly you should feel the chest muscles working.

Whether sitting, standing or walking, always hold the bosom up high, on a stretched diaphragm.

Waist Make it a regular accident to drop a tin of hairpins, or a packet of cigarettes and bend from the waist to pick them up. Whenever there is anything on the floor that needs picking up, keep knees straight and do a toe-touching bend to pick up. But only do this inside your own quarters because it isn't a particularly lady-like attitude, especially in service skirts.

Ankles Get the sitting-on-the-table habit, even if it does mean you won't be married this year. Maybe you won't ever be married if those ankles don't get slimmer.

So sit on the table and swing your legs from the knee—you can do it for hours and it does help the ankles.

Point the toe as you swing the leg outward, straighten as you come in.

All-over This is just a general figure former and posture helper. Lie perfectly straight in bed, on your back, and arms at side; stretch first the left leg as far down as possible, then relax it into normal position, then stretch the right leg. Alternate the leg stretching but let the stretch be felt down your whole side each time.

If you want to help your figure as you sleep, don't curl up into a catlike ball, but sleep with legs straight and body straight, on back, with head turned first to one side and then the other.

Hips From now on make the floor your most preferred sitting place. During those long evening talks brush yourself a nice clean place on the floor (without a cushion, but a spot of carpet won't hurt) and sit with your tail on the hardness of the floor clasping your knees in your arms. Rock backwards and forwards rhythmically, and, if you can manage it, from side to side. In the backward and forward movement, your feet will leave the floor while you go back and return to the floor as you come forward. You will feel pressure on those bulging places and know that it is a form of massage working the bumps off. Sit with hands clasping ankles and rock if the bulge is fairly low. Anyhow, once you get on the floor you will be able to feel where you are treating the superfluous and adjust it accordingly.

CHAPTER 5
MOTORING AND TRAVEL

Between 1919 and 1939, the number of cars in Britain rose from 109,000 to just under two million. With car ownership widespread, wartime conditions presented a number of challenges for motorists. The blackout made driving at night extremely dangerous and resulted in a significant increase in accidents, to the point where many motorists chose to drive only when there was a full moon. Not only were cars a danger to each other, but cyclists, pedestrians and particularly soldiers in camouflage uniform were almost impossible to see. Cedric Brudenell-Bruce, Lord Cardigan, a prominent car enthusiast, was the author of several motoring columns in the early months of the war, and although his theories were sometimes questionable (according to him, people with brown eyes had poorer night vision than those with blue eyes), there were also sensible suggestions rooted in his personal experience, such as following the white line painted along the centre of main roads, and painting the otherwise distractingly reflective back of headlamps a matt black. When official headlamp shields were introduced early in 1940, driving, albeit at limited speeds, became marginally less treacherous.

Petrol rationing had been introduced early, on 22 September 1939, with each motorist allowed between four and ten gallons a month. Petrol for commercial vehicles was dyed red making it off limits to private motorists. Drivers spent time tinkering with cars, fine tuning their car engine in order to make their vehicle run more efficiently and their ration last longer. Car companies brought out more fuel-efficient economy models and there was even a revival of ungainly 'gas bag' cars, first introduced during the First World War. But these efforts were to little avail when petrol supplies were stopped entirely in March 1942 for all except official war workers and doctors. Car owners were resigned to preparing their cars for a hibernation of unknown length and looking for alternative ways of getting about, a situation that saw a resurgence of cycling in Britain.

Driving Under Blackout Conditions
By The Earl of Cardigan

Britannia & Eve (November 1939)

The author of this article is of the opinion that to follow the white line in the centre of the road is the safest method of progression at night. The picture shows the obvious dangers of hugging the near side of the road.

The private motorist in wartime must needs be a creature of considerable hardihood. In the first place, he must so organise his journeys that the maximum amount of useful travel may be done with the minimum expenditure of petrol. Then, if he ventures on the roads after nightfall, he must exert very great skill if he is to keep going at any reasonable pace without risking a collision.

Already it is evident that, for drivers whose eyesight is only moderately good, the best advice as regards night driving is simply "Don't!" There are, I am sure, many thousands of drivers whose sight enables them to drive in daylight with perfect safety and efficiency, but who are not justified in being on the road after dark while artificial lighting is reduced to its present bare minimum.

Brown-eyed people are particularly unfortunate in this connexion. Their vision in daylight is often very good, but at night they are generally at a disadvantage compared with people of the blue-eyed type. This may perhaps seem an unfair dispensation of providence—but it is none the less a point which should be noted.

As to how to get along most efficiently and safely after dark, assuming really sound eyesight, opinion seems to vary very greatly. Some people claim that it is dangerous simply to follow the white line in the centre of the road; but, personally, I regard this as being almost the safest method of progression. The only obstacle likely to be encountered along a white line—if we may disregard the urban lamp-post—is another car which is being driven in a similar fashion.

If this other car is coming towards one's own, it is nearly always visible from a considerable distance. There is thus ample time for both parties momentarily to abandon the white line and to close in to the near side while they pass each other. If the other car is travelling in the same direction as one's own, there is still no real difficulty. The rate at which, in these days, one car is able to overtake another at night is exceedingly slow, so that again there should be more than sufficient time for the white line to be abandoned—one car drawing in to its left and the other out to its right.

Any alternative method of driving seems to me to have far greater possibilities of danger. If a driver keeps close to the left-hand kerb, he will continually come upon cyclists and pedestrians who are doing likewise, and will have either to brake suddenly or to swerve in order to avoid them. These sudden movements, especially if the road is wet, must always involve an element of risk.

The danger is particularly great in districts where soldiers are quartered. Khaki is intended to blend with the landscape—and by faint artificial light it does so alarmingly well. The very greatest care is needed wherever men in khaki are likely to be found in the roadway after dark.

In many respects, the wise driver can save himself anxiety and nerve-strain by choosing his route intelligently when compelled to stay out after dark. Nowadays it nearly always pays to keep to the main roads, even if this involves some extra mileage. All main roads now have white lines throughout their entire length, and this alone should be sufficient recommendation.

There are, however, other advantages. Main roads may be lined with trees; but the trees are generally so far apart that they do not completely overhang the road. It is seldom, therefore, that natural light (which exists to a small extent on any except a pitch-black night) is completely excluded from the central part of the main road.

Then, the best sort of main road may be lined by those small red or white reflectors which can be inset into stone kerbing or set into the road surface along the white lines. These little devices are quite excellent as an aid to wartime driving, and a real boon to motorists wherever they exist. Even a shrouded side lamp gives enough light for them to reflect, so that they show up as little white or red specks for some hundreds of yards ahead. Would that they were more generally employed!

Naturally, no such aids can be expected on side roads, so that a cross-country journey is both more hazardous and slower. Time is lost on the minor roads, nerve-strain is increased and petrol almost certainly is not saved. The cross-country route may be five miles shorter; but it will be found that numerous scares, false alarms and minor emergencies cause the driver continually to check his progress, probably necessitating the use of a low gear. Even if the car is kept in top gear, low engine speed with alternate acceleration and deceleration is by no means economical. The truly economical speed for a petrol engine is a steady speed, probably in the region of 30 m.p.h. in the case of an average saloon car.

In talking of roads, we must not, of course, ignore the human factor. The physical condition of the driver will always be of supreme importance, whether on a good road or a bad one. For example, it is obviously inexcusable to attempt to drive at any speed above a crawl if one has just come out into a dark street from a brightly lighted room.

A good many accidents, I fancy, could be avoided if considerations of this sort were kept in mind. The human eye needs a little time to adapt itself to strange conditions. After a short while in comparative darkness, it is able to give very fair night-time vision; but it needs to "warm up" to a task of this sort. Its efficiency rises after the first five or ten minutes, but may fall again through fatigue after an hour or more of work in a faint light.

However much care is taken, it is certain that driving under blackout conditions will never be pleasant, nor will it ever be entirely free from risk. Both the risk and the unpleasantness, however, can be greatly minimised where drivers take the trouble to develop what one may term a "wartime technique" to meet the new and difficult conditions.

Black-out Driving in Winter

By Our Motoring Correspondent

The Illustrated Sporting and Dramatic News (12 December 1941)

In spite of propaganda and in spite of experience, there remains a great deal of uncertainty about driving in the black-out. Neither drivers nor pedestrians show that appreciation of the problem which might be expected.

One example is worth quoting. A friend who has to do a great deal of black-out driving was complaining about his bad night sight. He was worrying about it quite a lot and complaining that it was a trouble which he had never before experienced. He asserted that he used to have particularly good night vision.

I made the usual recommendation of raw carrots, but without much hope of it affecting the position. Nor did it. He religiously ate all the things which the doctors say contain the vitamins which affect night vision, but he still found the greatest difficulty in night driving. At times it almost amounted to distress, and he had to stop the car and rest for periods during his night journeys.

One evening I happened to travel with him. His car has been "camouflaged" over, but it retains its large polished headlamps. And I noticed that the side lamps are situated in such a position that their light is thrown on the curved and polished backs of the headlamps. The side lights are dimmed in accordance with the regulations; but being near the reflecting surfaces provided by the headlamp backs, they throw back a certain amount of light.

The rounded back of each headlamp, in fact, was a point of light—not indeed bright, but noticeable. And when seen against the drab, dim background presented by the faintly illuminated road ahead, it kept forcing itself on the attention.

The suggestion was made that the backs of the headlamps should be painted over with matt paint or the lamps encased—except for the masks—in some dark material. The result was very satisfactory. The driver found that his black-out trouble had been greatly reduced.

That contains a lesson which ought to be broadcast to all those who, in the course of their war work, are bound to drive much at night, especially along country roads where the boundaries are ill-defined.

It is impossible to pay too much attention to ensuring that there is nothing throwing back even the smallest amount of light into driver's eyes. The side lamps must not throw their light on any part of wings or headlamps which is polished and liable to reflect back the light.

Brightness levels are the things that matter; not so much absolute amounts of light. A person distinguished a thing at night because parts of it have a brightness level distinct from the surroundings. If a point of light is constantly in the driver's field of vision, it will distract his attention and prevent him from seeing well ahead of it.

Soldiers as Pedestrians

I am really on the same subject when I appeal to all Commanding Officers to instruct their officers and men on the camouflage effect of khaki. The material is chosen precisely because it is difficult to see. In the black-out it is often impossible to see, and the soldier, walking beside the road, is usually distinguishable only by hands and face.

There is plenty of evidence which suggests that the soldiers themselves are entirely unaware of how well camouflaged they are during the black-out. They walk along the roads, sometimes two or three abreast, and seem to rely entirely upon drivers seeing them.

It would be an enormous help if the Ministry of War Transport would turn its attention to problems of this kind and ensure that information about them is widely disseminated. Such factual information would be much more helpful in promoting road safety than the parrot slogans about care and avoiding risks.

...

Winter Motoring in Wartime

By A. Percy Bradley

Britannia & Eve (February 1940)

War effects some astounding changes, not only for those who put on uniforms and become engaged in active service but also for those who retain their civilian dress and endeavour to carry on much as they did in peace time. Amongst the latter, motorists find themselves confronted with quite a new outlook on motoring. Before the declaration of war, when two or three car owners gathered together, fantastic stories as to how they completed journeys from one destination to another at average speeds of 50 m.p.h. or more were related. To-day, however, all that is changed and the deeds which are now considered worthy of mention would have been laughed at some months ago. A driver will now boast that his car does 55 or 60 m.p.g., and will not worry to any great extent as to the speed with which his journey has been completed. Fortunately for the British motorist the manufacturers, about eighteen months ago, took a lively interest in this question of petrol consumption, with the result that when war broke out there were on the market a large number of different cars which would travel astounding distances on one gallon of petrol. Naturally, with petrol being sold at greatly increased price and only a small ration being doled out, the average motorist is filled with an inclination to tune his engine, and particularly the carburettor, in such a way that the previous gallon will take him a greater distance than it ever did before.

Carburettors which possess adjustments that can be readily got at are a terrible temptation to the enthusiastic driver, but I would like to warn this individual that enthusiasm, praiseworthy as it may be, will not produce the desired results unless a certain amount of skill is displayed. I know from personal experience that the insertion of a smaller jet can produce surprising results, but frequently not in the direction desired, and once the maker's adjustment has been altered it is exceedingly difficult to put things back as they were, when the tinkering has proved disastrous. Provided a driver is satisfied not to exceed, say, 40 m.p.h. a carburettor can be turned by an expert so as to give a better mileage per gallon to a car. All the well-known carburettor manufacturers will give advice as to how their products can be adjusted to produce the desired results, and so, if the car owner will write to the appropriate maker, time will not be wasted. Better still, take the car to the carburettor maker's service depot or to some motor agent who is accustomed to deal with that particular carburettor.

Other parts of the car can receive attention in such a way as to improve consumption. For instance, tyre pressures should never be allowed to drop below those recommended, lubricants in the gear box and back axle should be as thin as is consistent with good oiling properties, and brakes should be so adjusted that they do not rub. Then again, if the car is allowed to coast down gradients and up to traffic lights which demand a stop quite a few additional miles can be covered to the gallon.

Motorists in these wartime conditions are now taking a keen interest in the moon, whereas in the piping times of peace only those of an amorous disposition worried very much about its rising and setting. I find myself fixing up dinner appointments which necessitate a journey of any length during the blackout hours only on those nights when there is a full moon. No doubt as time goes on all drivers will see more readily in the dark by reason of the accumulated experience of driving during the hours of darkness. Even now I think motorists are not nearly so worried as they were a month or two ago, though night driving has been made less onerous by the introduction of the new official headlamp shield. Provided that a driver is content to travel along at a speed not exceeding 30 m.p.h., the official shield on an average headlamp provides a reasonable driving light.

These shields must, of course, be fitted properly, otherwise the effect not only on the driver himself but on those who approach him in the opposite direction will be quite unpleasant. Considering that one can buy these shields so cheaply and in such a convenient form, there is no excuse for any motorist not having one fitted to his car in a proper manner. The well-known firm of Lucas supply a shield and lamp front rim all in one for lamps of their own manufacture. Fitting one of these is just child's play, for all that has to be done is to remove the front of the lamp with its glass and substitute the combined rim and shield.

Many motorists are apt to forget that with these shields and the other lighting restrictions that prevent their side lamps giving any useful illumination, their battery is being called upon to perform extra work, particularly during the winter months. Driving in towns and cities in the old days only meant lighting up the side lamps, but to-day, once it gets dark, the one shielded headlamp has also to be switched on. The unfortunate battery has thus a fairly thin time, but the drain on it is nothing compared with that due to the prolonged efforts of the self-starter to induce the engine to start firing in the morning on pool petrol. Batteries are usually tucked away under the back seat, under the floor boards or covered over under the bonnet, and just because they usually do their job without a murmur they remain unseen and forgotten. Under present conditions such forgetfulness on the part of the owner will cause a lot of trouble. They must be inspected and the level of the acid in each cell checked over, and brought up if necessary by the addition of pure distilled water until the top of the plates is just covered. Motorists may think batteries are tough, and so they are up to a certain point, but if they do not receive attention they will sooner or later show that they need it. Even if the car is stored away for the winter, or a longer period, the battery must not be overlooked. It should be handed over to some trustworthy local garage for attention whilst the care is laid up.

Under present conditions a driver should always keep his eye on the dashboard instrument which indicates whether the dynamo is charging or not. If the needle does not swing in the right direction a stop should be made at the first garage, or better still, at one of the many Lucas service depots so that an expert can ascertain the cause of the trouble and apply the necessary remedy. Should the battery prove to have run itself down to any extent, a service battery can usually be taken on board at these depots, whilst the owner's own is being recharged. I cannot plead too strongly on behalf of the car battery. It is a willing servant, gives efficient service and will not usually let down its owner, provided it is given a little attention now and again.

Laying Up Your Car? Some Practical Hints and Tips

By Alan Hess

Britannia & Eve (May 1942)

If any added proof were required of the topsy-turvy state of our present-day world, it would be found in the fact that June, this year, is the month in which hundreds of thousands of car owners will be reversing their pre-war custom.

Before the war this was the month eagerly awaited by large numbers of fair-weather-motorists to bring forth their cars from winter storage and, with the coming of warm days and long evenings, to put them into commission for five or six months of pleasure motoring.

Holiday tours were planned, and weekend jaunts and picnics arranged, for those were the blessed days of peace and plentiful petrol.

How sadly changed is the scene today.

Even those all-the-year-round motorists whose war work has necessitated continued use of their cars, will now be planning to store their trusty vehicles, as a

Lubricate with grease-gun and oil-can all parts requiring such attention

result of the Government's decision to abolish the basic petrol ration from the end of this month, and to make drastic cuts in supplementary allowances from now on.

Obviously there will be a number of motorists who, to save storage charges, will decide to *sell* their cars now, but I would advise readers not to adopt this course unless they absolutely must do so, as the market will not be favourable for them at such a time.

For the benefit of those who determine to lay-up their cars, the following hints will, I hope, prove timely.

In the first place, it must be remembered by those living in prohibited areas that, under the Defence Regulations, there are three main requirements which *must* be carried out.

First, the car must be properly immobilised. The ignition key as well as the distributor cover or rotor arm must be removed, labelled and handed in at the local police station.

Second, the car doors must be locked and, in the case of saloon cars, the windows must first be closed.

Third, care must be taken to ensure that the garage doors can be secured.

These three provisos *must* be complied with by motorists living in defence areas ; but both these and indeed *all* motorists contemplating the storage of their cars, will be wise to observe certain other precautions, in order to ensure that deterioration of their cars and of their accessories does not ensue through resultant inactivity.

Here, briefly, are some of the most necessary items to attend to:—

Wash, thoroughly dry and then carefully polish your car

BODYWORK—Wash, thoroughly dry and then carefully polish the car. Take particular care to ensure that the out-of-sight, underneath parts of the chassis are thoroughly dry; also the door and window apertures.

Brush out the interior of the body and spread covers over the upholstery and the floor rugs, sprinkling these covers with anti-moth powder. Make sure the sliding roof apertures are completely dry and that the roof is tightly closed.

Smear all plated parts with Vaseline and lubricate all hinges.

If your car is an open model, erect the hood, dust it with anti-moth powder and leave it with the hood up.

CHASSIS—Lubricate with grease-gun and oil-can all parts requiring such attention, notably wheel-hubs, springs, brakes, steering mechanism, shock absorbers and engine controls.

ENGINE—Drain the engine sump and refill with fresh oil, running the engine for a few minutes after doing this, to ensure proper circulation.

Then make certain that the water circulation system is completely drained and flushed through with fresh water until it flows out cleanly, free from traces of rust.

In order to protect the cylinder bores against rust, the Automobile Association advises car owners to take out the sparking plugs and pour into the top of each cylinder an egg-cupful of oil. When this has been done, the engines should be turned over on the starting handle to distribute the oil, and the plugs should then be replaced. Repeat this procedure every two or three months whilst the car is standing idle.

BATTERIES—No part of the car is more liable to deteriorate through inactivity than the battery. If the battery on your car is a new or otherwise good one, it will be well worth while to make arrangements with your local garage to store it for you and to give it a freshening charge every six or eight weeks.

If, on the other hand, the battery on your car is an old one, and the cost of this special maintenance is not worth while, disconnect the leads and wipe them free from acid, wrap their ends in rag and tie them firmly in such a position that they cannot inadvertently cause a short circuit. Also wipe the battery terminals clean.

TYRES—Do not leave the car resting on the tyres. On the other hand, do not rely upon hydraulic jacks to keep the tyres clear of the ground. Either leave the car supported by chocks placed under the axles, with the tyres clear of the floor, or adopt the less desirable course of leaving it standing on the bare rims after having removed the tyre covers and tubes (not forgetting the spare wheel), putting these away in some dark, cool, dry place.

In conclusion, do not forget that Lloyd's underwriters have agreed, as a special concession, to return to motorists laying-up their cars as a result of the withdrawal of the basic petrol ration, the full portion of their insurance premiums for the unexpired period of their policies from July 1 onward.

Take out the sparking plugs and pour into the top of each cylinder an egg-cupful of oil

How to Look After Your Bicycle

Britannia & Eve (August 1943)

More people than ever before are riding bicycles and liking it, but the enjoyment of cycling depends much upon the ease with which the machinery runs. This, in its turn, depends upon the proper care and maintenance of all the working parts.

To run easily and without breakdowns, a bicycle has to have regular attention. Not necessarily elaborate attention, but regular car and an occasional overhaul.

Clean machinery works smoothly, so it should be a rule never to put a bicycle away muddy and wet. Rust and corrosion creep up on you quickly and jam the parts unless you make a ritual of wiping over the frame and the machinery after riding in dirty weather.

Easy motion and freedom from punctures largely depends upon keeping tyres well inflated. Slack tyres make hard work of riding and are far more susceptible to sharp points on the road surface. The rubber situation and the conservation of tyres make it a duty to keep them in good condition anyway, quite apart from comfort.

Mending a puncture is a simple operation. The trickiest part is removing and replacing the outer cover, which a child can do after a little experiment.

The rest consists in getting out the inner tube, inflating it and holding every part in turn under water until bubbles indicate the perforation of the rubber.

Make a pencil mark round the spot. Dry the rubber and clean it with a small piece of fine sandpaper, rubbing very softly over the place.

Apply sticking solution and let it get tacky before putting the patch on. Give it time to dry, then deflate the inner tube, replace it inside the outer cover and get this also back within the rim of the wheel. Inflate hard and the job is finished.

Regular oiling at essential points is vital to the smooth working and the long life of all the parts. Don't wait until the machine begins to run hard before getting to work with the oil can. Make a regular operation of it.

The illustration shows the main points for oiling. Don't swamp the parts but make a principle of lubricating little and often.

The bicycle chain should be removed every few months for cleaning. To do this prise off the spring clip which can be found on the detachable link. Remove the plate at the side and draw out the detachable link.

When the chain is removed, clean it thoroughly with a brush in a bath of paraffin. Drain off the paraffin and oil the chain at every link. Hang it up to drain off the surplus oil before replacing the chain on the machine.

Faulty brakes are a danger to life—yours and other people's—and need careful handling in use, as well as regular care when out of use. Use brakes gently when riding. The habit of jamming brakes on hard on every occasion wears down the linings and puts on unnecessary strain on the cable. Regular oiling of all the visible nuts which hold the brake mechanism together is very necessary in wet weather.

If you buy a second-hand bicycle it is a wise precaution to take the brakes to a mechanic for cleaning, oiling and adjustment before you use the machine.

Keep chromium surfaces dusted and dry them when you come in out of the wet.

These small attentions take very little time if they are carried out regularly but add so much to the efficiency and comfort of riding.

K.L.

CHAPTER 6

SUPPORTING THE WAR EFFORT

In tandem with efforts to manage the nation's diet was a campaign to 'dig for victory' and produce vegetables that would supplement rationed foods. The phrase, first coined in the Evening Standard newspaper, was then used in a leaflet produced by the Ministry of Agriculture and Fisheries in November 1939, asking for half a million allotment holders for the Grow More campaign implemented by the government. Before long, vegetable plots were taking over front gardens, back gardens and every available patch of land (even the tops of Anderson shelters), inspired by official 'Dig for Victory' posters bearing the striking image of a gardener's boot pushing down a garden fork. A series of 'Dig for Victory' leaflets helped novice gardeners, as did radio programmes such as 'Gardeners' Question Time' and 'In Your Garden' featuring the famous Cecil Middleton, who was to wartime gardening what Lord Woolton was to food. Magazine articles gave additional printed information on how to dig and fertilise soil, sow and tend to plants and how to maximise yield by inter-cropping. Vegetable growing became the main preoccupation of many, and for food that was not eaten immediately, there was always the option to preserve or pickle for leaner months. Gardening also had the side-effect of promoting neighbourly cooperation as people shared advice and produce.

This is what "Digging for Victory" Really Means

By Our Horticultural Correspondent

The Illustrated Sporting and Dramatic News (6 December 1940)

The basis of success in growing vegetables is a deeply cultivated soil which contains sufficient humus to provide the foods necessary to plant life. These two factors are so closely related that it is practically useless to make provision for one without the other.

Deep cultivation is necessary to aerate the soil and to promote the activity of the bacteria which it contains. It is this soil bacteria which makes the plant food soluble so that the plants can easily assimilate it. Deep cultivation is also necessary to ensure good drainage, to allow the roots of plants to penetrate to their maximum depth and to encourage the upward rise of moisture to replace that lost by surface evaporation.

Surface moisture is necessary to ensure seed germination and the feeding of the shallow roots of young seedlings; evaporation of this moisture can be considerably checked by constant hoeing between the crops, thus forming a loose mulch of topsoil and conserving moisture underneath. The addition of humus-forming material assists in improving the texture of soils, rendering light ones retentive of moisture and heavy ones lighter and more easily workable. Soils containing humus are dark and quickly absorb the sun's rays and become warmer than those which lack humus.

Ordinary routine digging of ground which has been well cultivated for a number of years consists of simply turning it over to a depth of one food (or one "spit" as it is commonly called). But this will not meet the needs of the people who are taking up vegetable growing for the first time—in many cases on unbroken pasture land.

"A PLACE FOR EVERYTHING"—: A well-ordered tool shed is the trade-mark of efficiency. Clean your tools each time after use and wipe them over with an oiled rag.

If the plot to be cultivated is meadow pasture, ordinary digging will not secure sufficient depth of loose soil to satisfy the essential needs of their crops. Two alternative methods can be followed. The first is deep trenching, or digging three feet deep, but I do not recommend this method to the beginner for it involves very laborious work and there is the possibility that unfertile or sour subsoil will be brought to the surface and the top layer of good soil buried under it.

Shallow trenching and double digging to a depth of two feet is, in my opinion, the best form of cultivation for the plot of ground with which we are concerned. The procedure is a perfectly simple one:

Stretch two garden lines two feet apart across the plot at right angles to its length. Take off a strip of turf between these lines across the width of the plot, cutting the turves to such a thickness that all the fibrous grass roots are attached. The turf need not be cut to any particular shape as it will be chopped up and buried. Wheel the turf to the opposite end of the plot. Take out a trench two feet wide and one foot deep across the area stripped of turf. Wheel the soil from this trench to the opposite end of the plot, placing it in a heap reaching across the width. Step into the trench and fork up the bottom of it to a depth of one foot.

Filling the Trench

To fill in the trench move up the first garden line at the beginning of the plot and stretch it two feet in front of the second one and parallel with it. This will mark the area of the second trench. Strip the turf from this area, chop it up into pieces about two or three inches across and throw it into the bottom of the first trench. On top of the chopped turf place the manures and other material necessary to make up for deficiencies in the natural soil.

WORK IN PROGRESS: This ground has been cultivated, but, except for turf stripping, it is being dealt with as described in the accompanying article. Note convenient method of stacking manure.

A WELL-MANURED TRENCH: The manure is spread evenly over the bottom, and will be covered by "top spit" from the next trench, the area of which is marked by the garden line.

TURNING OVER THE TOP SPIT into the previous trench, which has been double dug and manured.

Next take out one foot of soil from the second trench, turning it over on top of the manure in the first trench. This will completely fill in the first trench. Fork up the bottom of the second trench, cover it with chopped turf from the top of the third trench, fill it with manure and top-soil and proceed with this routine until the end of the plot is reached. The last trench is filled with the turf and soil moved from the opposite end when operations began.

The soil on the surface of the plot, particularly if it is heavy, should be left as rough and lumpy as possible, to allow for full exposure to air and frost which pulverizes and sweetens it.

Natural manures are difficult to obtain these days, but if possible your choice should be governed by the nature of your soil. For heavy soil use strawy horse manure, for light cow or pig manure. These should be spread evenly over the bottom of the trench, on top of the chopped turf, about two barrow loads being used for every square pole of ground.

Failing natural manure, spent hops (obtainable from breweries) make very useful humus-forming material, whilst decayed vegetable refuse and rotted leaves contain the elements of plant food in considerable quantity.

A TRENCH 2 ft. by 1 ft. deep has been made, and the digger is making the bottom another food deep.

SOIL FOR THE LAST TRENCH is wheeled forward after being taken from the first trench. The pneumatic-tyred wheelbarrow makes the work easier and does not cut up the ground and paths.

If you are dealing with pasture or neglected land which is badly infested with docks, thistles or other weeds having long tap roots great care should be taken to remove and burn such roots from the top spit before turning it into the trench. When the land is exceptionally dirty it is sometimes better to stack the turf long enough for the perennial weed roots to decompose and use it subsequently as a top

DUMPING SOIL: To finish off the job it is conveniently tipped across the width of the plot.

dressing. If perennial weed roots are buried they are bound to be a source of trouble for many years.

Very heavy soils can be greatly improved by mixing sand, wood ash, lime and brick rubble with them, though this treatment must usually be continued for several seasons before appreciable results are noticeable.

The soil of pasture land is generally infested with wireworm, wood-lice and other pests. A sure remedy is horticultural naphthalene applied at the rate of two ounces per square yard. Fork it just under the surface after the digging operations have been completed.

The sooner your new plot is broken up the better. The initial work is hard and may be tiring to the beginner. Take it easy and don't overtax your strength until your muscles become acclimatised to it. On the thoroughness with which the first digging is tackled will depend the success of your subsequent efforts.

VALUABLE MATERIAL: The heap on the left is short strawy stable manure, and this is supplemented by well-rotted grass mowings (right) which have accumulated during the previous summer.

Intensive Vegetable Production: Inter-cropping as a War Time Necessity

By Our Horticultural Correspondent

The Illustrated Sporting and Dramatic News (2 August 1940)

Anyone of average strength and intelligence can dig a piece of ground, manure it, sow it with seeds and produce a reasonably good crop of vegetables. I suggest, however, that for our war effort we should not be content until the maximum yield of which our garden, large or small, is capable has been secured. To attain this goal our operations must be so planned that two crops of vegetables and in some cases even three are taken each year from as large an area of ground as is practicable. This procedure is known as intensive cultivation and calls for skilful planning and forethought; indeed, the measure of its success might almost be taken as the test of a really good gardener.

At White Waltham Place, near Maidenhead, there is a fine garden owned by Mr. L. Oppenheimer where these intensive methods have been brought almost to a fine art. I recently spent a most interesting time there with the head gardener, Mr. F. Berry, and was greatly impressed not only with the practical methods of inter-cropping which he adopts, but also with the fact that his methods are not carried so far that quality is sacrificed to quantity. The photographs reproduced on this page will, I think, amply confirm this.

FORMAL GARDEN AND LILY POOL: The ornamental vine (*Vitis purpurea*) growing on the pergola is a very attractive feature of this "garden within a garden."

EVERY INCH USED: Good gardening like this will do much to make this country self-supporting as regards vegetables.

MAIZE (OR INDIAN CORN): A lesser known vegetable which increases in popularity every year. Attractive in appearance, it can in these times take its place in the formal flower garden. It is raised from seed sown in a heated greenhouse and transplanted outdoors early June. "Golden Bantam" is one of the best garden varieties.

PEAS IN PLENTY: These fine rows of peas will be succeeded by root crops for winter storage. The peas are started on twigs, and then 2 foot wide large-mesh wire netting is used as support.

The secret of success in intensive vegetable production is deep cultivation, a well-enriched soil, and the arrangement of inter-cropping so that the secondary crop (or catch-crop as it is usually called) does not restrict the development of the major crop. The following are typical examples of successful inter-cropping, most of which, though not all, are practised at White Waltham:–Lettuces, carrots (stump rooted varieties), or spinach grown on the ridges between celery trenches—cauliflower or lettuces between rows of tall peas—beet between currant and gooseberry bushes—parsley sown very thinly at intervals in the onion bed (it is said that this is a deterrent to the dreaded onion fly, though I cannot vouch for it)—colewort cabbages (the small rosette variety for winter use) or radishes between rows of tall growing brassicas—lettuces grown close to the runner bean rows.

In regard to successional cropping during the summer, the sowing or planting of a number of vegetables for autumn and winter use may be made as soon as crops of early peas and early potatoes are cleared. These include any of the winter greens (savoys, kales, broccoli, etc.) which have already been raised in a separate seed bed, also turnips, garden swedes, French beans, winter onions and spinach. If early potatoes are succeeded by autumn cauliflower, a third crop may be grown on the same ground by following the latter with spring cabbage. Another favoured site for the spring cabbage bed is ground just cleared of onions as it is firm and in good heart after the careful preparation usually given to the onion.

The interplanting of potatoes with brussels sprouts and other brassicas is a matter of some controversy as, if the potatoes are planted at the normal distance of 2½ ft. between rows, the haulm may impede the growth of the Brussels, particularly in a rainy season. This method, however, finds an advocate in Mr. Berry, at any rate during the present emergency, and he overcomes the objection mentioned by spacing the potato rows at 3 ft. apart. The usual routine of hoeing, feeding and mulching is, of course, doubly important where such heavy demands as outlined above are made on the soil, but the effort is well worth while at this garden as I am told that all the surplus produce is given to hospitals.

I realise that this is only touching the fringe of a very extensive subject and I shall no doubt return to it during the great seed sowing offensive next spring. Many further examples of inter-cropping could be quoted. The chief consideration to bear in mind, however, is the suitability of one crop in relation to its neighbour, the important factors to allow for being:—

1. Habit of growth (compact or spreading) of both top vegetation and root run.
2. The needs of the plant in regard to sunlight or shade.
3. Free circulation of air between crops.

Overcrowding is not intensive cultivation; get the most out of your garden by all means, but give everything a fair chance.

WHITE WALTHAM PLACE: A stately approach to a country house. The well-kept grass enhances the beauty of the surrounding flowers.

THE WOODLAND WALK: A delightful place for a stroll when the thermometer reaches the 80's.

MASS PRODUCTION: Human ingenuity assisted by Nature produces two or three successive crops on the same piece of ground each year. This picture shows lettuce (just planted), summer cabbage, parsley, climbing French beans, lettuce, celery and runner beans, and is typical of many similar plots at White Waltham. These crops will be succeeded by others, as described on this page.

POTATOES AND WINTER GREENS: There is every indication of good yields from both. The potato haulm is partially cut off soon after it is in full flower.

A WINTER FAVOURITE: A fine batch of early brussels sprouts. Rich, firm soil and a long season of growth essential to turn out such good plants. Seeds were sown early in the year, and later batches will ensure a long picking season.

RUNNER BEANS. At 4 weeks to 8 weeks and 12 weeks, to give a succession. The 12 weeks rows, almost hidden, are being picked. Note the wide spacing, 20 inches between the plants, which means better beans and just as heavy a crop as more crowded plants would produce.

Eggs were not rationed, but mainly because the supply of them could not be guaranteed and the government was reluctant to ration any food that could not be consistently available. Dried eggs were a poor substitute for the real thing and so keeping chickens became more popular. The same applied to rabbits, which were relatively easy to look after and could provide meat as well as fur pelts. Even bee keeping was taken up by increasing numbers. 'Apis' in a March 1941 issue of Britannia & Eve announced that, 'Makers of hives are working like the busy bees themselves for never has there been such a boom in bee-keeping.' Elsewhere people kept ducks, goats and even pigs (pig owners could benefit from being members of the Pig Keepers Club). Livestock naturally added to the daily tasks required of the housewife. Hens needed feeding, cleaning out and careful husbandry to ensure they lay as productively as possible. There was also the risk of the family growing attached to animals, and finding both the mental and physical strength to kill an animal that had become a family pet, was one of the most upsetting things to negotiate for householders who had no previous experience of raising livestock.

The Lays of the Land

Britannia & Eve (September 1941)

Are you one of the stoics who have listened to friends rhapsodising about their home-laid breakfast egg each morning, with a rather superior air of indifference? Maybe, by now you are in the mood to pocket your pride and become a hen-keeper yourself. Not for the love of hens—but because hens have sufficient oomph to lay an average of five or six eggs a week when they are on top of their form.

There are three choices before you this month. Six-month-old pullets that will start laying immediately. Last year's hens that will lay again after Christmas, with luck—and lay for a year. Or two-, three-, four- or five-month-old pullets. Work out that pullets generally start laying when they are six months, and you will know how long, respectively, you will have to wait before you find your first egg.

This year it may be a case of get what you can. Egg and fodder rationing has curtailed the hatchings, and you will find the young pullets costing quite a lot. If you do get very young pullets be most particular about rearing them—mix cod liver oil with their mash in cold weather, if you can still get it.

The most popular, easily obtainable cross-breed is the Rhode Island Red crossed Light Sussex. These birds are good layers; they are not too heavy or clumsy when it comes to hatching out a brood—yet they are a good size for putting in the oven when they come to the end of their egg-laying career. The time for them to turn into one good meal is after they have laid for two years before their second moult period in the case of hens, and from four to six months if having brought up a sitting of chickens, you fatten the cockerels for the table.

You will need 4 square feet per bird for an intensive hen-house, the flooring of which can be either earth or wood covered with litter. This is the smallest space possible. The house should face away from the winter winds; the fixtures—perches, nests and food and drinking vessels—should be kept very clean.

Make certain that the drinking water is well out of the way of any droppings. Have a droppings board under the perch, keep the nests away from the perches, and have a good bunch of greens hung up so that the hens must reach, or even jump to get their beak full. The nests should be large enough for a full-sized hen to turn in, and you should have one nest to each three hens, even if they do all queue up for the favourite. You must have food utensil, grit utensil, drinking vessel, dust bath, perches, and droppings board in the hen-house. If you have a run, the eating and drinking utensils are outside, and the hens will make their own dust bath. Get really heavy or well-fixed troughs and vessels that will not spill or turn turtle easily.

Food is the axle on which the happiness of hen and keeper turns. In peace time one meal a day was grain, one meal mash. These days it will be two mash meals for most hens. You can make pseudo-grain by putting moist bread scraps through the mincer. The pressure and the moisture will make them come out like little worms of bread, mince them straight on to a tin tray and bake them in this shape; they will be just like grain and your hens will eat them with relish. As for the mash, it can be practically anything except bad tinned food, rhubarb or rhubarb leaves, and coffee grounds. Sometimes you should add greens to your mash.

Everything should be put through the mincer, then boiled until it is well cooked. The additional balancer meal is then put to the mash and this should bring it to a very dry consistency. A wet mash is very bad for the hens. Lawn cuttings will do very well for greens. Raw swedes or turnip will add the precious vitamins in winter. Fish and meat scraps are invaluable, but make sure you don't give your hens too much fat, because this will put them into a condition that is not conducive to laying.

If any of the hens are weakly, try feeding them with cod liver oil or milk; if they are sick give them a fountain-pen filler of castor oil (you will need help for this); if they are over-heated, a weak solution of Glauber salts. If the yolks of the eggs are too pale it indicates that your hens need a little more meat or proteins. If the yolks are too vivid a yellow it means that they are having too much of this type of food. If the egg shells are soft or not properly formed see that the hens get more grit. If a hen is sneezing and watery-eyed you can dip its whole head in a weak solution of some disinfectant—Izal or iodine (a teaspoonful to a half a gallon).

Colds will travel and sometimes prove fatal. If one hen is definitely weak or ailing, cut your losses and off with its head. Broody hens are those which, overcome by motherly instincts, sit on their nests all day, refusing to lay. Catch them as soon as possible and put them in a coop that has slats of wood for the floor, the uprising draughts will discourage them from sitting, and they will lose their longings for a family and become layers again.

---

8 a.m. or earlier. First feed of the day—mash or grain substitute, 5 oz. per bird. Clean water. See that grit bowl is full. Clean droppings board in intensive house.

12 a.m. Green scraps.

5 p.m. The mash; hot in winter, it can be cold in summer. Keep varied in flavour if possible. Collect eggs.

Weekly. Thoroughly cleanse hen house, scrape and scrub droppings board. Scrub out all the eating and drinking vessels. Clean dust bath, and put shaking of good insecticide in them. Add a very weak solution of permanganate of potash to the drinking water.

Monthly. Repaint at least the perches with a mixture of 75 per cent paraffin to 25 per cent creosote. The entire interior of hen house should have been painted with this a few days before the advent of the hens.

Like Rabbits?

Britannia & Eve (February 1942)

This is the month in which you should start your year's rabbit breeding. Two does can provide you with about thirty-five to forty rabbits in the year (allowing four litters of about five per litter each) if you start early. Rabbits like breeding in the sunshine, and in the months starting from now you will find much free fodder in the lanes and weeds of the country.

Food   The average amount of food needed daily by each adult rabbit is 2 oz. of well-balanced foods per pound live weight of rabbit. All garden waste, pea haulms, grass, dandelions (not too many) can be utilised for food. If you remember that potato foliage, raw potatoes, rhubarb, onions and any mildewed greens or frosted root vegetables are poison to rabbits, you are fairly safe.

Hogsweed is a great favourite from the lanes, and you should try and make hay from the garden lawn or lane sides in the summer, for the winter. Plan to keep four does next winter and you will get an allowance of bran mash for them. Learn to make a pot mash of scraps for them much as you would for hens—potatoes and potato peelings, and all the scraps of the kitchen will suit them well. You can give water if you like. There are two divergent schools of thought on this subject, many never giving their rabbits anything to drink at all.

Accommodation   Single hutches should be 3 feet by 2 feet by 1 foot 9 inches. Double or breeding hutches should be two single hutches joined together and a doorway cut in the common side. The breeding side should have a front wooden door while the other living compartment should have a front wire-mesh door; both doors should open so that it is easy to clean the hutch floors out thoroughly when necessary. Every second day is the usual time.

During the winter months keep the floors covered in straw, or deal sawdust. In the summer you need only have straw in the breeding compartment.

Varieties   Favourite for flesh is some variety of buck crossed with a Flemish Giant doe, or Belgian Hare doe. Many people think that the Belgian Hare rabbit (although certainly not a hare because hares will not breed with rabbits) has too strong a flavour, in which case it is wise to keep to the Flemish Giant, and have a good Old English or Silver Grey buck.

Your rabbits should have bright eyes, short claws, sleek well-groomed coat, white teeth, and a fairly dry nose—never buy a rabbit that is suffering from a wet nose or snuffling; and look into the ears for signs of canker.

Breeding   When ready to be placed with the buck the doe will show signs of excitement, although it is not always necessary to wait for this because, if the doe is ready, the mating will take place after she has been with the buck for a few minutes. If this does not take place, you will have to take her away and put her back with him in a few days' time.

Never put the buck into the doe's hutch, as she may, if not ready, attack him viciously. If the mating is successful she will make her nest in two or three weeks' time (allow her plenty of hay for this), and this should not be disturbed. The litter should arrive thirty-one days after mating. If it is necessary to examine the litter do so on the second day, after rubbing the hands well with a little of the hutch hay, and then leave well alone.

The young should stay with their mother for four weeks in the breeding months, although the last litter can stay for eight weeks.

After the first three litters the doe is ready to breed again when the young have been removed, providing she has been well fed all the while. She should have plenty of drinking water, and if possible a little milk when feeding her young, and should have maximum rations from the beginning of the second to the beginning of the fourth weeks, as this is her most trying period.

Watch the young carefully for signs of cold and any eye congestion, bathe the eyes if there are any signs of discharge; another complaint that is rather common is pot-belly, caused by overeating greens, so change their diet at once. The average amount needed by young rabbits separated from their mother is about 1 oz. of concentrated food per day with a liberal supply of grass, hay and green stuff. You can keep lots of about six young rabbits together until the age of three months, when the bucks and does should be separated.

Does are ready for breeding at six months and bucks should be ready for killing at that age or even earlier—a well-fed buck of the Flemish Giant strain will be ready for fattening at four and a half months if he has had good rations.

Pelts Can be cured roughly at home. Scratch the pelt and tack it tightly stretched on to a board and scrap with sharp knife to remove any fat. Keep in a dry place and sponge daily with a mixture of alum and water (12 oz. of boiling water on 4 oz. of alum). Hang up to dry for a week and then pumice for a few days until it is soft. It is always advisable to have the pelts cured at a specialists, rather than finish them at home, because, incorrectly treated, the skins can give the wearer a form of dermatitis.

Bees: Mainly for the Beginner

By "Apis"

The Illustrated Sporting and Dramatic News (28 March 1941)

Makers of hivers are working like the busy bees themselves for never has there been such a boom in bee-keeping. The demand for hives and appliances can still be met, but there is going to be an acute shortage of bees. In his article in our February 28th issue "Apis" explained how the beginner can get his stock of bees—by buying a complete stock, a nucleus (3 or 4 frames with a young fertile queen) or a natural early swarm.

Last month I gave you, the would-be beekeeper, some advice on how to get your bees. Now comes the problem of the best beehive and where to place it. A hive may be double-walled or it may be single-walled, and there are various types of each.

A double-walled hive should certainly be chosen in any cold, exposed location, but a single-walled, which, of course, is cheaper, may give sufficient protection in a warm and sheltered one; even there I should always prefer the former type, if the extra expense is not an objection. The W.B.C. hive, which is made to hold ten "British Standard" frames, is the one in commonest use in this country and is a very good pattern for the ordinary amateur.

The great objection to it is that modern queens are a good deal more prolific than the old British black bee, for which this hive was designed, and this amount of comb space is no longer sufficient for her majesty to rear as large a family as she would like. She finds her house too small for her requirements, and, as she cannot enlarge it, her only remedy is to remove with half her family into another one (which we, of course, call swarming).

Early Swarms Out of Fashion

The old-time skeppist delighted in an early swarm ("A swarm of bees in May is worth a load of hay"), but the ambition of the modern bee-keeper is to avoid all swarming, which upsets the work of the hive and greatly reduces the harvest.

So more room must be allowed somehow, and this can be done in the W.B.C. hive by placing on the top of the first brood box a second similar one or one to hold 10 shallow frames. Or else the brood box may be made four inches deeper, so as to accommodate frames 12 inches deep instead of the usual 8 inches. Other hives are made to take 15 frames of the usual size, but these and others which take much larger frames all involve heavier weights to lift, and had best be avoided by the weaker brethren.

Timber is now very scarce, so don't delay choosing your hive and placing your order. While waiting for it to arrive, have a look round for the best spot to stand it, both best for the bees and sufficiently convenient for yourself when working it. For the benefit of the bees the spot should be sheltered from the wind, dry and sunny; if it faces south or south-east, this will be all to the good, but that is of less importance. For your own convenience there should be enough room to move easily all around it, and it is advisable to have it where an issuing swarm is likely to be noticed.

Just one or two "don'ts." Don't put the hive so that the bees fly straight out over a public path or highway, unless there is a fence high enough to make them rise above the traffic. Don't have long grass or weeds growing in front of the entrance. Don't put it where an inquisitive cow may knock it over; this would be quite as upsetting for the cow as for the bees, so fence off the hive if it is in a field where horses or cattle are grazing.

Getting Them into the Hive

Well the hive arrives, is given a couple of coats of paint and placed on the appointed spot. Then at last the great day comes, and buzzing with excitement the bees put in their appearance. Naturally, if you have never handled bees before, you are probably feeling quite a little anxious as to what is going to happen when the lid comes off the box, and some thousands of excited bees are free to do their worst. Just keep cool and go about the job quietly, and you will be surprised to find how easy it is, and that the bees are quite harmless and friendly.

Stand the box in some dark corner where they will not be disturbed, and leave them to settle down till well on in the afternoon. Then give them a good feed of warm syrup (about 5 or 6 oz. of sugar to a ¾ pint of hot water). A strip of flannel may be soaked in this and laid on the wire gauze above the bees, keeping it constantly wetted as the bees taken down the syrup. Finally put on your veil and light the smoker, and, taking with you a frame of foundation, carry the box to the hive.

Now take your courage in both hands and gently remove the lid. You will be relieved to find that few of them will fly, none will show any desire to sting and all of them will set up a contented hum of thankfulness at finding themselves at liberty again. That at least has always been my experience, and I have never yet found it necessary to use either veil or smoker. But these give the beginner greater confidence, and he will be armed against trouble in case he should make mistakes and rouse a few tempers.

Transferring Frames

The frames may now be lifted one by one and placed in the same order in their new abode. Then put in the frame of foundation and finally the "dummy"; cover them up warmly and put them on the roof. Any stray bees remaining in the box should be shaken on to a board in front of the hive. The fearsome job is then finished, and next day the bees will be found to be taking their bearings and already getting to work.

While you are transferring the frames, if the afternoon is a mild one, see if you can spot the queen. The frames will not be very thickly covered with bees, and it should not be too difficult to find her. She can be easily recognised by her long, tapering abdomen, and her long legs, which give her a markedly different gait from the rest. If she is of a very placid temperament, you may see her carrying on her normal life, poking her head into the cells to see which are empty and fit to have an egg laid in them. But usually she will be pushing her way through the workers trying to escape from the glare and publicity. If the bees are Italians, she will be somewhat different in colour from the others, which makes her still easier to find.

But don't keep the frames exposed if there is a chilly breeze; if you do the young brood may be chilled and die. The bees should be fed regularly and further frames of foundation given them as required; then in five or six weeks you should have a fairly strong colony of bees, ready to do their job when the honey flow starts.

Work for April.—Clean propolis (the sturdy substance gathered from the barks of trees by the bees to use as cement) and burr comb off the tops of the frames and scrape the bottom boards clean. If the stores are at all short, give a little syrup every evening to encourage brood-rearing but avoid giving so much that the queen is hampered by lack of egg room.

A "TELESCOPIC" W.B.C. HIVE of the type described in the article. This one, made by Taylors, of Welwyn, is open to show the arrangement of the frames and sections.

STORING THE HONEY: This picture shows a section (a small square honey comb), a shallow frame and a broad frame. The queen is kept from reaching the shallow frames and sections and it is from these that the honey is taken.

THE SMOKER: Like the veil, the smoker gives the beginner confidence when taking a swarm.

Bees and Fruit Tree Spraying

In fruit-growing areas, accidental injury to bees sometimes occurs through the use of poisonous sprays, particularly those containing arsenic. Simple precautionary measures are:—

1. As far as possible, spray only during these two definite periods: (a) before the blossom buds open; (b) immediately the petals have fallen.

    It is realised that different varieties of fruit trees blossom at varying periods, but every effort should be made to avoid indiscriminate spraying of open bloom.

2. Do not place beehives in orchards until early varieties of fruit are actually in bloom.
3. Remove the beehives from the orchards before "calyx" spraying, *i.e.*, directly after petal fall.

Beekeepers who contract to place bees in orchards for pollinating purposes should remind fruit-growers of the danger to the bees through spraying or dusting open blossom.

The Second World War triggered a huge, coordinated recycling effort, with almost every conceivable piece of waste saved in order for it to be transformed into something useful for the war. Waste paper and cardboard (even Christmas crackers) could be pulped and turned into fuses, targets and containers for shells and explosives. Bones were used in the making of nitro-glycerine, a key ingredient in explosive devices; rubber was needed for all sorts from gas masks to barrage balloons, and rags became gun wadding, uniforms, ground sheets, tents and fuse cloths. Almost all kitchen scraps became food for pigs and hens, which in turn became food themselves. 'Save every infinitesimal scrap of paper', ordered *Britannia & Eve* in its July 1942 issue, while poster campaigns urged the public to save metal, which could make tanks, while 'salvage saves shipping' or 'waste paper goes into action' were other frequent reminders. Ever practical, *Britannia & Eve* helped savers and salvagers by giving ideas about how and where to store their scrap until it could be collected.

Salve It

Britannia & Eve (February 1942)

Things which are too often repeated become boring. Think of good jokes.

Well, you have heard so much about paper salvage in the last few months that you might quite likely be bored. Nevertheless, it is our intention to nag you still more about salvaging every possible scrap of paper that passes through your hands. For every scrap counts, and counts vitally.

Think of this. Perhaps the man you want at your side more than anybody in the world at this moment is dependent on your help. He may one day be standing behind a tank or gun or operating the cannon of an aircraft that won't answer back at the enemy, not because there are no shells, but because there are no shell cartons.

Shell cartons seem pretty unimportant perhaps, but shells have to have cartons. It's not just that the munitions people like to tie them up pretty, but they do like them safe. They like them protected and they like every single shell to reach the men behind the guns as it was sent out from the factory—perfect.

So shells have to have cartons, and the paper for those cartons has got to be found. Some of it by you.

Besides these vital shell cartons, the paper you save goes back into pulp and reappears later as gun fuses; as interior components for mines; as dust covers for aircraft engines which have, at all cost, to be kept clean; as cut-out targets for firing practice, and as washers for every kind of mechanism that needs washers. One ton of waste paper makes 140,000 washers. If you have medals at arithmetic, see how many washers one pound can make. And it wouldn't take long to salvage a few pounds. Think of the weight of some of those old magazines that are cluttering up your shelves.

Paper-saving isn't a new sort of parlour game. It is a grim and vital objective. It is a realistic contribution to the efficiency of our fighting forces. Remember that the next time you drop your bus ticket on the pavement instead of putting it in the salvage box provided.

Carry your salvage campaign beyond the obvious measures of not using the whole morning paper to light the fire with and not burning all your old receipts and papers. If you must light the fire with paper, use only the very dirtiest and greasiest paper around the house. If you live in the country go out and collect fir cones. Dry them for kindling instead of paper. Wood shavings are just as good if you can find a timber yard.

You don't have to line cupboards and drawers with paper. Keep them well scrubbed instead. Hold on to every single paper bag that comes from the tradesmen, and by removing the food immediately keep it in sound condition for return to the shop. Stop using face tissues and keep little huckaback towels for cleaning off make-up. Stop laying sheets of newspaper down after you have washed over the kitchen floor.

Don't overlook the old books, the old files, the old love-letters you thought you wanted to keep always. Bring them out for salvage.

Curb your letter writing impulses. Keep correspondence down to essentials and instead of writing all the local scandal to Cousin Emma in Devonshire, tell her on a postcard that you are well and chalk up another shell carton to your credit. If you must write letters, use every inch of paper. Write smaller. My maiden Aunt was born before her time. She used to write all down the page and then write across it at right angles. There was no paper shortage then, but Auntie had a bee in her bonnet about waste. We could use the same sort of hat ornament to-day.

Stick economy labels over old envelopes and don't let any remnants of pre-war pride trip you up about this, either. Some people think that a war economy label on an envelope is as good as a family crest.

Corral your odd pieces of waste paper by hanging up a bag or an old pillow-case in the kitchen. Put every scrap into it.

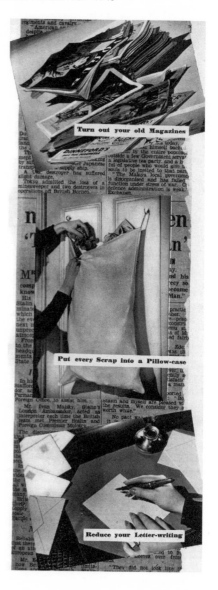

Turn out your old Magazines

Put every Scrap into a Pillow-case

Reduce your Letter-writing

SOURCES

CHAPTER 1

"Life below Stairs" *Britannia & Eve* (November 1940)
"Fuel Facts" *Britannia & Eve* (February 1942)
"No Maid? No Matter!" *Britannia & Eve* (August 1943)
Winifred Lewis, "Home Savers" *Britannia & Eve* (February 1942)
"Minor Repairs" *Britannia & Eve* (November 1944)
"War Law at Home" *Britannia & Eve* (February 1940)
"Harmony in One Flat" *Britannia & Eve* (February 1943)
"Wedding in a Hurry" *Britannia & Eve* (May 1944)
"Passed by the Censor" *Britannia & Eve* (October 1942)

CHAPTER 2

Jean Burnup, "Dress" *Britannia & Eve* (September 1942)
Jean Burnup, "Dress: 1 into 2, 2 into 1" *Britannia & Eve* (October 1941)
"New Clothes from Old Discards" *Britannia & Eve* (May 1942)
Vere Denning, "Beg Borrow or Steal" *Britannia & Eve* (November 1940)
"We're on the Mend" *Britannia & Eve* (August 1941)
Vere Denning, "Care for Clothes" *Britannia & Eve* (February 1940)
"Dry Clean at Home" *Britannia & Eve* (October 1943)
"Repair Your Own Fur Coat / And Now For Your Raincoat" *Britannia & Eve* (October 1944)
"Knitting for the Long Winter Evenings: Warm Woollies" *Britannia & Eve* (October 1943)
"No Coupons Needed" *Britannia & Eve* (November 1942)
"Make Yourself these String Slippers" *Britannia & Eve* (January 1944)
"Leather Permitting" *Britannia & Eve* (September 1944)

CHAPTER 3

"Off the Ration Book" *Britannia & Eve* (February 1940)
"It's In the Cooking" *Britannia & Eve* (September 1943)
"Vegetable Variety" *Britannia & Eve* (January 1943)
"Queer Fish" *Britannia & Eve* (January 1943)
"Out-of-a-can Cookery" *Britannia & Eve* (January 1942)
"Out of the Hedgerows" *Britannia & Eve* (July 1944)
"Food for the Winter Store" *The Illustrated Sporting and Dramatic News* (12 June 1942)
W. P. Pycraft, "Edible and Medicinal Seaweeds" *Illustrated London News* (27 January 1940)
"Wartime Dog Foods" *The Illustrated Sporting and Dramatic News* (25 December 1942)
"Lunch in the Office" *Britannia & Eve* (January 1941)

CHAPTER 4

CHAPTER 5

CHAPTER 6

All the articles in this manual were sourced from Mary Evans Picture Library, which has been supplying historical images to a wide range of users since 1964. The library covers all periods and all genres through a mix of photography, illustration, fine art and ephemera, drawing on their own unique archive, as well as over 350 different contributor collections ranging from personal family photograph albums to internationally-renowned heritage institutions. The content for Home Front Manual was specifically taken from magazines in *The Illustrated London News* archive which is housed and managed at Mary Evans. The archive consists of nine different publications, all of which were published weekly and include *Britannia and Eve, The Sketch, The Illustrated Sporting and Dramatic News*, and of course the flagship title, *The Illustrated London News*. The team at Mary Evans are dedicated to curating and making available images and articles from this incomparable visual record of the past century and a half. To find out more about Mary Evans Picture Library visit www. maryevans.com.